# STRATEGIES FOR TEACHING ENGLISH LANGUAGE, LITERATURE, AND CONTENT

MARY LOU MCCLOSKEY     JANET ORR

LYDIA STACK     GABRIELA KLECKOVA

WAYZGOOSE PRESS

*Strategies for Teaching English Language, Literature, and Content*

Copyright ©2018 by Wayzgoose Press

Written by Mary Lou McCloskey, Janet Orr, Lydia Stack, and Gabriela Kleckova

Illustrations by Brandon Kruse http://www.brandonkruse.com

2018 edition edited by Dorothy Zemach

Cover design: DJ Rogers; cover image by Brandon Kruse.

05

All royalties from this publication will benefit The Global Village Project: http://globalvillageproject.org

# CONTENTS

# INTRODUCTION

*Strategies for Teaching Language, Literature, and Content* is designed to support grade level teachers, content teachers, and English for Speakers of Other Languages (ESOL) teachers who are working with learners of English in many different contexts.

**Strategies** are methods and plans for delivering instruction and promoting learning. We see strategies as versatile instructional tools that teachers–and learners–can apply with a wide variety of materials and instructional goals. We believe that acquiring facility with a range of strategies prepares teachers for diverse teaching and learning situations.

We offer in this book 51 strategies that support active, interactive, and integrated language development. The research-based strategies are designed to increase both learner motivation and learner success. Student engagement in and interaction with all kinds of texts and experiences from literature and content areas are supported and directed toward learning. Most of the strategies also integrate language modes of listening, speaking, reading, and writing to build language fluency, accuracy, and comprehension.

We have organized the guide into five sections:

1. **Strategies for New Learners of English** includes 11 strategies for oral and written language development for newcomers to English;

2. **Strategies For Building Comprehension Before, During, and After Reading a Text** offers multiple ways to help learners prepare to read, search for meaning as they read, and explore a text in depth after they read;

3. **Reading Process Strategies** includes seven different ways to structure the actual reading of a text to bring variety, interest, and depth of processing as learners read;

4. **Graphic Organizers for Text Structure** offers a variety of visual tools to show how text is organized and how it works and to promote oral and written discourse around text;

5. **Vocabulary Exploration and Study** includes a baker's dozen strategies to explore words and learn their meanings.

Each of the 51 strategy descriptions includes an example of the strategy in use. Our goal is to illustrate how the strategies are flexible and versatile enough to be used with, and to enhance, the content your students study. We hope these tools will expand your teaching repertoire in ways that make English language teaching and learning rewarding in your classroom.

*Mary Lou McCloskey*
*Janet Orr*
*Lydia Stack*
*Gabriela Kleckova*

# PART I

# STRATEGIES FOR NEW LEARNERS OF ENGLISH

Newcomers to English have unique needs. They often experience a "silent period" during which they are developing and understanding language but not yet comfortable producing the new language. The strategies in this section are designed to support newcomers and to promote a comfortable entry into their new language. Most of these strategies integrate speaking, listening, reading, and writing. This offers learners who are literate in their first language opportunities to use their knowledge of the written word in learning a new language, and provides support for students acquiring their first literacy in English to develop the skills and strategies of English literacy (McCloskey, 2017).

The section includes these strategies:

1. **Adapting Oral Language to Increase Comprehension:** Teachers can adjust the way they

use English to make the language comprehensible and inviting to new learners.

2. **Culturally Responsive Instruction:** Connecting to learners' previous cultural experiences provides learners with respect for their own identities that makes learning more meaningful and engaging.

3. **Total Physical Response:** Actions combined with language have been shown to increase learning. TPR is a versatile strategy for developing comprehension and can move into speaking and reading.

4. **Chants, Songs, Poetry, and Raps.** Rhyme, rhythm, and repetition make language memorable and encourage learners to create their own discourse by varying within the patterns.

5. **Language Frames:** Learners use frames to practice important phrases and patterns of the language, and to learn ways to participate in academic talk.

6. **Guided Reading:** Learners develop reading skills and strategies through small-group instruction using books that gradually increase in difficulty.

7. **Shared Reading:** Teacher and students use a shared large-print text (on chart, big book, or screen) to develop reading skills and strategies.

8. **Shared Writing:** Teacher and students read a shared text together, while they discuss and develop elements of writing.

9. **Language Experience Approach:** Learners and teacher write together about a shared experience, then use the text they have created for reading and writing.

10. **Vocabulary Introduction and Practice for Newcomers.** Teachers are offered a range of principles and tools to select important vocabulary and help learners acquire those terms.

11. **Dipsticking: Checking Comprehension for All Learners Frequently.** Teachers use a variety of strategies for quickly and frequently checking comprehension of all learners in the class as part of daily teaching.

# ADAPTING ORAL LANGUAGE TO INCREASE COMPREHENSION FOR NEW ENGLISH LEARNERS

The way we use oral language can make a big difference in how well students understand us and are able to build proficiency. Here are a dozen suggestions for using our own language to help our learners:

**1. Articulate clearly:** Avoid blending one word into the next. We naturally compress language a great deal in oral American

English, so we need to be self-aware about it. Learners will do best when we pronounce sounds clearly but naturally, and separate words rather than blending them.

> **No:** *What...is...your...name?* (Speech is too slow to be understood.)

> **No:** *Wachername?* (Although we do this in conversation, it will be hard for learners to hear the words.)

> **Yes:** *What is your name?* (Language is natural, but clear)

**2. Face students:** Watching the mouth positions and movements of a speaker provide extra clues to the language. Make sure that you stand so your students can see your mouth and facial expressions to aid learners' comprehension.

**3. Use pictures, gestures, and realia** (real things to see, handle, and talk about). Pictures, things, and actions are very helpful cues to meaning for newcomers. Use these whenever you can to accompany language you use with beginners. You can guide learners to use their own things (e.g., school materials), create their own pictures, or imitate gestures and actions for learning. Do you think you can't draw? An excellent resource is *1000 Pictures to Copy for Teachers*, by Andrew Wright (1985).

**4. Increase wait time.** Recall your own experience learning another language. It takes time to process oral input in a new language. Provide that time by waiting before you ask a student to respond. We tend to be uncomfortable with quiet seconds in class, but they are much needed to give ELs time to think. The normal wait time in a classroom is only about 1-2 seconds, but with practice you can learn to be comfortable with more.

Researchers have found that increasing your wait time to 5-7 seconds will give many more learners time to respond. So, be comfortable with a little silent time after a question. Count slowly to 5 or 7 or whatever time is needed until most students are ready to respond.

Also remember that if you call on the first student who raises a hand, you will tend to spend most of your time speaking with the most proficient learners. Let learners know that you will nominate responders rather than getting a show of hands. For example, keep sticks with student names on them in a can on your desk so that you can randomly nominate a student to respond while others respond mentally.

**5. Paraphrase often.** Watch learners' faces carefully and notice when they are not with you. When needed, re-explain instructions or explanations in language ELs are likely to understand.

**6. Explain or rephrase idioms and figurative language.** Idioms are a fun and interesting part of our language, but they are difficult for beginners to understand. Idioms can make the comprehensible incomprehensible, but they are not used very frequently. Be aware of your use of idioms and figurative language, so you can explain them when needed, and limit their use. Think before you use phrases like these, and determine if it is valuable to spend the time explaining and demonstrating them: *Piece of cake. Chip on your shoulder. Fly off the handle. In your face. Smell a rat. Burn the midnight oil. Bad hair day,* and so on.

**7. Connect new language to what learners know.** Language is more comprehensible if students start with the known and move to the unknown. So, to learn something abstract like measurement, have learners begin by measuring their surroundings and/or writing their own recipes. If they are learning the geography of countries and continents, begin with

your students' or their families' countries and continents of
origin. If they are learning about money, have them come up
with problems about making change from their own experience
shopping for things they need.

**8. Use direct and simplified sentence structures and
adjust vocabulary with beginners**. Active voice (*You will put
your homework in this box.*) is easier to understand than passive voice
(*Homework will be placed in this box.*). Sentences with many clauses
are complex and difficult. A few simple sentences (*First, multiply or
divide. Go from left to right. Then, add or subtract. Go from left to right.*)
are more comprehensible than a complex or compound sentence
(*When solving a mathematical expression, remember to multiply and divide
before you add and subtract, and to perform the operations from left to right.*)
When possible, explain concepts using high-frequency, commonly
used terms. When you need to use low-frequency, more technical
terms, provide explanations and demonstrations. Also consider
translation: sometimes translations are the fastest way to help
learners comprehend new words, so use or have students use a
translation dictionary or online translation when available and
needed for key terms.

**9. Highlight key ideas and vocabulary.** Learners can only
take in so much information at a time, so focus on the most
important information and omit unnecessary elaboration. Really
think about what is most important in what you teach—not just
what is in the textbook. Highlight important ideas and terms by
stressing the words in oral language, writing the words on the
board, pointing out words, putting them on a word wall or in
learner dictionaries, and through repeated, meaningful uses of
the terms.

**10. Check comprehension frequently.** Keep in mind that
students are not eager to tell you that they do not understand.
Because they respect you and want to be seen as learning, many

times students will watch you and nod their heads as you speak, while they comprehend very little. So you will not find out what students get by asking, *Do you understand?* but by asking for specific responses. See "Dipsticking" for more ways to check comprehension.

# CULTURALLY RESPONSIVE INSTRUCTION

English is the most widely learned additional language in the world, but contexts and purposes for learning English vary widely. English may be taught to students as an official national language in a context where many languages are spoken (e.g., South Africa or Nigeria), as an international language to be used as a common language across many cultures (e.g., in Europe, or in a refugee camps), or as a new language in an English-speaking context (e.g., the USA, Canada, or Australia).

Students may learn English for:

- Internal political reasons–English provides a common means of communication
- Economic reasons–English for international business or trade
- Practical/political reasons–advantages of English for employment or to immigrate to a country where English is spoken
- Intellectual reasons–access to academic texts and the Internet in English
- Historical reasons–English is a legacy of imperialism of an English-speaking country
- Entertainment reasons–English is the language of much popular music and media

Many of these contexts also involve introducing learners to new cultures and classes combining students from multiple cultures. For these reasons, we propose making English culturally responsive to both new cultures and to the cultures students bring with them (Nieto, & Bode, 2012). Culturally responsive instruction looks much deeper than just celebrating the food, holidays, customs, and clothing of the cultures of learners. It involves family relationships, communication styles, values, and attitudes that learners bring to school. Cultures are the ways, the regularities of particular groups of people, but they are not static–culture is fluid and ever-changing. Teachers of newcomers have the opportunity to set the tone, to start learners on a successful path; and culturally responsive instruction is a key tool.

Culturally responsive instruction includes these five features:

**1. Communication of high expectations for all learners.** Achievement can be undermined by subtle factors, including racial, ethnic, and gender stereotypes. It is the responsibility of teachers to be ever striving to address and overcome their own stereotypes in order to build social bonds, high expectations of learning, and students' high expectations of themselves.

**2. Creation of an affirming cultural context.** The goal for English learners is often *acculturation* (the ability to live in a world viewed through two sets of cultural lenses) and not *assimilation* (trading one culture for another). Teachers have the power to affirm the cultures of learners and the responsibility to learn as much as possible about them.

**3. Culturally responsive instructional practices.** These practices include

- incorporating different cultural perspectives into the curriculum
- seeking out materials that portray the diversity of learners
- learning about students' cultures and languages to enhance instruction
- actively promoting equity and mutual respect
- developing classroom routines that incorporate how students respect one another, get to know one another, and treat one another in the English language classroom culture.

Practices should also include ways to motivate all learners to participate, communicate that everyone can learn at a high level, assess students in ways that are valid for their language proficiency and cultures, and challenge learners to strive for excellence.

**4. Cultural mediation.** In order to provide culturally responsive instruction, teachers must seek to become cultural mediators by increasing their own personal knowledge about diversity. This means they might

- explore their own personal histories and that of the groups they belong to
- believe that difference is the "norm"–that no one group is more competent than any other
- learn about the histories of the groups in the classroom
- learn how culture affects the teaching process
- help students learn about their own cultures and to appreciate the cultures of others
- adapt instructional practices to accommodate the different learning styles and strengths of learners in the classroom
- avoid judgments that might negatively impact the achievement gains of students

**5. Connection to homes and families.** There is very strong research evidence of the link between parent involvement and school-aged learners' success in school (Bennett, 2004) that make it essential, when we work with learners in this age group, for us to try to connect with our students' families. Yes, we have language barriers: parents in a new culture, speaking a new language, may be hesitant to participate in school events. We must therefore take the initiative in employing strategies for connecting with the home such as:

- finding opportunities to talk to parents informally

- sending home newsletters with information about school (translated into languages of families)
- using home/school folders to facilitate communication
- using email and telephone to communicate with families
- visiting homes and home communities to learn more about families and their cultures
- inviting parents to volunteer in the classroom
- inviting parents to school to showcase student accomplishments, introduce concepts such as bedtime reading, or explain the report card
- visiting local community centers and neighborhoods to learn more about resources and norms

In addition, it's important to make parent conferences as effective as possible, by

- providing translation as feasible
- organizing work samples that illustrate learning
- having clear notions about what will be communicated
- monitoring nonverbal signals, which are very powerful— use such techniques as eye contact, nodding while listening, and peer-to-peer seating arrangements
- listening carefully to parents
- avoiding placing blame on the family or making judgments
- conveying an attitude of acceptance, care, and concern

# 3

# TOTAL PHYSICAL RESPONSE (TPR): LEARNING LANGUAGE THROUGH ACTION

In the 1960s, James Asher developed a teaching method he named Total Physical Response. TPR helps students learn a new language through performing physical actions in response to commands. Asher's lessons, modeled after children's first language acquisition experiences, have been adapted for use with all ages.

Asher's lessons followed seven basic steps (Asher, 1996):

**1. Preparation.** The teacher prepares a short script, incorporating level-appropriate language and often using props and actions that help communicate the language. Asher recommends that teachers introduce only a few new concepts at once and wait until these are mastered before adding more.

**2. Demonstration.** The teacher and/or a few individuals demonstrate the actions for the series of commands. The teacher makes every effort to keep the lessons lighthearted and fun. The series is repeated several times with variations in the order of the commands.

**3. Whole group demonstration**. Now the whole group participates in repetitions and variations of the sequence.

**4. Written copy.** For students who are beginning to read and write in English, the teacher provides a written text, which students copy and study.

**5. Oral repetition and questions.** After listening comprehension has been completely internalized, students will begin to repeat the commands. These students are ready to begin to speak and to give the commands to their peers to follow. They can practice repeating the series, ask and answer questions about it, and respond to the commands out of order.

**6. Student demonstration.** Depending on language and reading levels, students recite or read the script and perform the actions in front of the class. You could also have learners make a video for later viewing and practice. The teacher checks carefully, and guides students toward correct pronunciation, grammatical usage, and comprehension.

**7. Pair practice.** Students solidify their learning by practicing in pairs, taking turns in roles as readers/speakers and actors.

**Effective adaptations of TPR** are a valuable part of a language program, particularly at beginning-level stages. Students benefit from the opportunity to listen first before being expected to speak, from the engagement that physical activities provide, and from the spontaneity of the action-oriented lessons. Teachers can build TPR scripts from language and procedures students need–anything from "sharpening your pencil" to "procedures in the chemistry lab." Remember to make the activities fun by including light-hearted and unexpected commands (but still using key vocabulary), for example, *Write the word on your hand.* or *Pat yourself on the back or Give your partner a high five.* Activities that can be adapted for TPR lessons include:

- pointing to pictures and other visuals on board or posters or in textbooks, board picture books or wordless books
- classroom routines and procedures such as coming to class prepared, checking homework
- manipulating letter, picture, or word cards
- map activities, science experiments
- math processes with examples

Here are some TPR routines:

## Workout

*Put your left hand in the air.*
*Put it down.*

*Put your right hand in the air.*
*Put it down.*

*Put both hands in the air.*
*Put them down.*

*Put your left foot in the air.*
*Put it down.*

*Put your right foot in the air.*
*Put it down.*

*Put both feet in the air!*

## How to Wash Your Hands

*Turn on the water.*
*Wet your hands.*
*Turn off the water.*
*Put soap on your hands.*
*Rub your hands all over.*
*Sing a song for 30 seconds.*
*Stop rubbing.*
*Turn on the water.*
*Rinse your hands.*
*Turn off the water.*

*Shake your hands.*
*Get one towel.*
*Dry your hands.*
*Use your towel to open the door.*
*Throw the towel in the trash.*

## Watch a Soccer Game

*It's time to go to the soccer game. Put on your jacket*
   *and hat.*
*Climb up the bleachers.*
*Sit down.*
*Our team just scored a goal. Stand up and yell, "GOAL!"*
*The other team is making a corner kick. Look scared.*
*It didn't go in. Sigh in relief.*
*You're hungry and thirsty. Go to the concession stand.*
*Point to the soda and popcorn.*
*Pay your money.*
*Go back to your seat.*
*Oh, no! The other team just made a goal. Cry.*
*Oh, no! A forward fell down. Look worried.*
*She's okay. Smile.*
*Our team scored again! Yay! Jump up and down!*
*One minute left.... Yay! We won! Clap!*

# 4

## CHANTS, SONGS, POETRY, AND RAP

Music is motivating to most learners of English. Starting as infants, humans are drawn to the joy of tunes, rhyme, rhythm, and repetition. Learners memorize songs from the radio, TV jingles, and raps they hear. This kind of language is often memorized as "chunks" of language that are not analyzed by learners word-by-word but memorized as groups of words.

Chants, songs, poetry, and rap can all be powerful learning for beginning learners. It helps them use the language in a pleasurable way immediately, feel part of a group, and ease into the complexities of pronunciation, intonation, and rhythms of a new language. And eventually, learners can be encouraged to analyze the language to understand the meaning and structure, and incorporate elements into their own speech and writing

With younger learners, songs (like *The Wheels on the Bus*) are often used with gestures and actions that help show the meaning. A chant activity such as *Going on a Lion Hunt* uses gestures that teach and reinforce prepositions like *over*, *under*, *around*, and *through*. Examples of these are easily found on YouTube by searching for the title.

Teachers use chants to reinforce content concepts, for example, Rutherford, 1998, p. 122:

> *For perimeter of a figure, you add the sides*
> *Add the sides, add the sides,*
> *For perimeter of a figure, you add the sides*
> *All the way around.*
>
> *(Sung to the tune of "Wheels on the Bus")*

Chants can be written to teach a particular language form, such as questions, pronouns, and tag answers, as in *Are You French?*, the question and answer jazz chant by Carolyn Graham (Oxford 1993) that begins like this:

| **Group A** | **Group B** |
| --- | --- |
| Are you French? | *No, I'm not. I'm Italian.* |
| Is he Korean? | *No, he's not. He's Japanese.* |
| Is she Spanish? | *No, she's not. She's Venezuelan.* |
| Are they Indonesian? | *No, they're not. They're Taiwanese.* |

Note: The chant above can be adapted to include the languages of students in your class.

On he first day of school, a teacher might introduce key vocabulary or language patterns with a TPR rap that includes pointing to the objects in the room.

### First Day Rap

*Show me a pencil.*
*Show me a pen.*
*Show me some paper.*
*Show me your friend.*

*Point to the window.*
*Point to the door.*
*Point to the table.*
*Point to the floor*

*Raise your hand high.*
*Take it down.*
*Show me a smile.*
*Never a frown.*

Teachers and learners can use songs written to help learners remember key concepts and can write their own chants to reinforce concepts and vocabulary they are learning, and then perform them with finger snapping, toe tapping, or clapping. For example, a class that is studying the metamorphosis of a butterfly might use the chant below, while students take turns holding up pictures they have made showing each stage of metamorphosis:

## Metamorphosis Chant

*The egg is on the leaf*
*The egg is on the leaf*
*The caterpillar hatches out*
*The caterpillar hatches out*
*The caterpillar eats and eats*
*The caterpillar eats and eats*
*The caterpillar spins a chrysalis*
*The caterpillar spins a chrysalis*
*Out comes a butterfly*
*Out comes a butterfly*
*The butterfly lays an egg*
*The butterfly lays an egg*

Or, a class studying the Universal Declaration of Human Rights might agree on the rhythm of a chant and then have partners each write the particular chant for each one of the rights:

## Bill of Rights Chart

Number 1:
    We are all equal.

Number 2:
    All people
    of all countries
    of all colors and
    all religions
    have these rights.

Number 3:
    All people have the right
            to live
            to be free
            to be safe

Number 4:
    No one can treat you as a slave
    You cannot treat any one else as a slave.

# 5

## LANGUAGE FRAMES

Language frames (Bunch et al., 2003; Dutro & Kinsella, 2010; Fisher & Frey, 2008; Jacobson, Johnson & Lapp, 2001; Kress,

2008) are effective tools for developing and scaffolding academic language functions and vocabulary for language learners. They can be used at each level of language development to guide learners toward more effective and sophisticated language.

Language frames are partially constructed cloze statements (statements with missing words/phrases to complete) that highlight the language and syntax needed for a particular language purpose.

Teachers can create frames for whatever language they are teaching and use them to provide learners with practice with the language structures while they develop and use language for their own purposes. Frames can be constructed to use the key signal words that indicate transitions and relationships in academic writing, to show such concepts as sequence, change of direction, illustration, cause or result, special relationships, conclusion, inexactness, or emphasis. They can thus be tailored to support learners in using the key language and structures of each content area.

Language frames can be taught using the Gradual Release of Responsibility Model (Pearson & Gallagher, 1983). Early on, the teacher takes responsibility for the lesson, modeling and explaining the frame; then the teacher supports students in using and practicing the skill; then students work with one another to use the skills, and finally students are able to use the language forms and constructions independently, without the frames. Language frames can also be constructed to be progressively more challenging as learners' language develops.

| Language Frames for SPEAKING | | | | |
|---|---|---|---|---|
| Topic: Functions of Organisms in the Ocean Ecosystem | | | | |
| 1: Entering | 2: Beginning | 3: Developing | 4: Expanding | 5: Bridging |
| This is a [beluga whale]. It is a [consumer/ producer]. | This is a [beluga whale]. It is a [consumer/ producer]. | This is a [beluga whale]. It is a [consumer/ producer]. | This is a [beluga whale]. It is a [consumer/ producer]. | This is a [beluga whale]. It is a [consumer/ producer]. |

The chart provides examples of language frames for English learners as they develop through language proficiency levels such as those described in WIDA (e.g., https://wida.us or the Common European Language Framework [http://www.englishprofile.org/the-cefr.

In science, students are studying ecosystems and working to understand the functions of organisms within ecosystems. Sample language frames are in the area of speaking.

## Examples of the Use of Language Frames in Content Areas:

**Language Frames for Science:** Clark County (Nevada, USA) School District [http://ccsdssl.weebly.com/up-loads/1/8/1/3/18139151/science_sentence frames.pdf]
**Language Frames for Math:** Math Frame Wiki: [https://mathsentenceframes.wikispaces.com]
**Language Frames for Social Studies**: North Clackamas (Oregon, USA) School District: [http://www.nclack-.k12.or.us/sites/default/files/fileattachments/instructional_ser-vices/page/49763/social_studies_explain_-_describe_sentence_frames.pdf]

**Language Frames for Language Arts:** Language Frames for Different Types of Academic Writing from Elgin (Texas, USA) ISD: [https://sites.google.com/site/elginisdellinitiative/documents/sentence-stems-paragraph-frames]

**Literacy How Academic Language Function Toolkit** (Adapted from Kate Kinsella) [http://literacyhow.com/wp-content/uploads/2013/06/Academic-Language-Functions-toolkit.pdf]

**Signal words from the US Literacy Information and Communication System:** [https://lincs.ed.gov/readingprofiles/Signal_Words.pdf]

# 6
## GUIDED READING

Guided reading (Fountas & Pinnell, 2016; Clay, 2001), or
Reading Workshop, is a model of literacy instruction that

involves a teacher and a small group of learners working at similar reading levels. While the teacher reads with a small group, the other students are engaged in independent or group literacy tasks. The approach requires strong planning and organization on the part of the teacher, but can provide instructional support to learners at a variety of stages of literacy development.

High-quality books are carefully, progressively leveled to introduce new reading strategies, vocabulary, language structures, and concepts of print gradually and effectively.

*Before reading*, the teacher accesses background knowledge, builds schema for the text, and previews the text with the learners. They may take a "book walk" through the text to make predictions and ask questions.

*During reading*, students read independently while the teacher monitors decoding and comprehension, and notes areas of strength or weakness. The teacher may prompt students to use a strategy they know, encourage them to re-read a passage, or point out a new text element.

*After reading*, the teacher checks learners' comprehension by discussing the text with the learners and encourages learners to return to the text for evidence to support their statements about it. Learners may do extended reading activities related to the text during their group meeting or independently. Texts are re-read many times to build fluency level before students move on to more difficult texts.

# 7

## SHARED READING

Shared reading is a strategy designed for entering/beginning
language learners (Holdaway, 1989; Wells, 1986; Allen, 2002).

Learners are engaged and are able to fully comprehend the text being read.

Teachers use a large text on a chart, big book or projection that all learners can easily and clearly see. Texts are at learners' instructional level and are frequently used to introduce texts that learners will read independently later. A session might look like this:

**Warmup.** The class warms up by reading together texts they have read before and are familiar with. These might be former read-aloud texts, language experience stories they have written, or TPR scripts they have used.

**Pre-reading.** The teacher conducts pre-reading activities, which might include a picture walk through the book, development of background knowledge, or helping learners make connections between the text/topic and their own experience

**Introduction.** Teacher introduces the text, talking about the parts of the book, the author, the illustrator, and how to turn the pages.

**Multiple readings for different purposes.** Teacher conducts multiple readings of the text, each time pointing to the words as they are read, and moving from teacher responsibility toward student responsibility. At first the teacher reads the text aloud. Later, learners are encouraged to read along with repeated language. Eventually, learners read on their own (or perhaps recite the story from memory if they are not readers yet.).

**Discussion and close reading.** Teacher leads a discussion of the book, including text elements, text structure, and key vocabulary/ideas, all depending on the genre of the text. Learners are sent back to the text to look for evidence to support ideas they have about it.

**Extension.** Students participate in extension activities, which might include listening to the text on audiotape with follow-up activities or assessment; creative expression and writing activities based on the text; and using the pattern of the text to create original texts.

# 8

## SHARED WRITING

Shared writing (Levine & McCloskey, 2013; Routman, 2014, 1994) involves collaboration between teacher and students to create and refine a text. Shared writing helps learners develop interest in and enjoyment of writing while they learn the purposes and skills of a variety of genres.

**Begin with a shared experience:** a story, a walk, a visitor, an item in the news, a unit of study.

**Build background.** Teach/review key vocabulary. Teach the structure and signal words of the genre. For example:

- *Narrative* may use a chronological sequence with present and past tense and answer questions such as what, when, where, and why.
- *Compare/contrast* writing will use signal words for things that are alike, such as *both, like, and, in the same way, still,* or words for things that are different, such as *however, but, yet, on the other hand.*
- A *procedure* might be in the command form with steps in a list and include words like *first, then, finally.*
- An *argument* might include a statement of position and supporting evidence.

All of these forms of writing can be adapted for the vocabulary and language level of the learners.

- **Brainstorm** the content on a graphic organizer.

- **Draft**. Have learners help you draft. They might dictate while you scribe, or work in pairs or alone to draft assigned sentences based on the brainstorming.

- **Read the draft together** and collect ideas about how you might revise.

- **Revise the writing together**. Use this opportunity to teach a few key elements of writing: grammar of verb agreement or tense; conventions of print such as capitalization, punctuation, and layout; elements of writing such as voice or word choice.

• **Put the piece to work as a reading and language arts text**. Duplicate or have learners copy the work in their notebooks. Encourage them to read it aloud to family, guests in the classroom, or one another.

# 9

# LANGUAGE EXPERIENCE APPROACH

The Language Experience Approach is particularly valuable for getting to know students and helping them tell their stories.

There are six basic steps in the approach (Meyerson & Kulesza, 2010):

**1. Students and teacher share and discuss an experience.** This might be a picture, a walking trip around the school, a book, a game, a video clip, or an event in the community.

**2. After the discussion, the teacher elicits language from individuals or the group.** The teacher writes learner ideas on a chart or the board for all to see, using the words of learners. When learners need vocabulary, teacher can help provide it, assuring that the group understands the meanings. The writing may make use of writing frames that have been part of previous instruction.

**3. The teacher and students read and revise the writing together.** The teacher occasionally reads back the dictation, asking if it is what the student intended, encouraging the student to suggest changes to improve the piece. In the context of taking dictation, the teacher can teach and reinforce such relevant skills as the vocabulary, letter sounds and patterns, conventions of print like capitalization and punctuation, word endings and parts, and important "mortar" or signal words.

**4. The text becomes a reading text.** The teacher and students read and re-read the text together. The teacher reads, the class reads in chorus, individuals read with others or the teacher, and individuals may read independently. LEA texts can be collected and made part of the classroom library. They can be kept as a diary of important class events throughout the year.

**5. The teacher and learners use the piece in follow-up activities**, which might include cloze activities, writing activities, ordering words or sentences from the story; writing original stories using the same structure, etc. Activities can be differentiated by student level. The text can be duplicated or copied by students to use for independent reading, and for selecting and practicing important vocabulary.

- Beginning students might search for certain words and underline them, read the story in chorus, or participate in an oral cloze activity.
- Intermediate students might unscramble sentences, choose words to enter into their journals, or match sentence strips to sequence pictures from the story.
- Advanced students might use the piece for silent reading, reading aloud, classification activities using vocabulary from the piece, and studying grammatical forms in context.

# 10

# VOCABULARY INTRODUCTION AND PRACTICE FOR NEWCOMERS

The suggestions below are for helping learners at the entering and beginning levels of English language proficiency to acquire essential early vocabulary. The words that are important for these learners are the highest frequency words—the first 2000 words make up about 80% of the words in any text, so it is beneficial to focus on these words, as well as words they need to function in school and to begin to learn the academic work at their level (Cobb, 2015; Levine & McCloskey, 2013; Nation & Waring, 1997).

Learners cannot simply learn to read the frequency list, however—that is not the way vocabulary is acquired, especially at early levels. They must first learn orally what the words mean. Importantly, many of the most frequently used words (e.g., *the, be, to, of, and, in, for, not, with,* and so on) are the most abstract—so this vocabulary needs to be introduced in context, as part of language chunks or frames, so that learners can acquire the meanings.

Oral development of vocabulary is supported by:

**1. Starting small.** Target a few words/phrases and provide learners with success. Providing adequate wait time to process new language will include all of your learners in the lesson, not just the ones who move quickly.

**2. Starting without expecting learners to speak.** Many learners are uncomfortable speaking at first but can acquire a lot of language through listening, acting, pointing, sorting, and playing games.

**3. Teaching frequent words.** Teach the most commonly used words, but also include some of the words to comprehend classroom expectations and content. For example, when introducing your classroom expectations, use actions, pictures, and a few words; but you might include one important principle using an academic word, such as *concentration, attention, participation,* or *cooperation*.

**4. Providing rich context and plentiful comprehensible input.** This includes using the language in chunks in a meaningful context, providing gestures, facial expressions, realia (real things), actions, and pictures that add meaning.

**5. Checking frequently for comprehension.** Use the tools of *Dipsticking* (see Strategy #11) every few minutes to check if learners understand. This will help you fine-tune your lesson to reach every learner.

**6. Matching your language and expectations to learners' language levels**. With entering students, use gestures, repetition, expectations for actions to show comprehension, and encouragement to participate in group chants, songs, and choral responses. Model all expected behavior. With beginning students, ask questions that can be answered by *yes/no* and either/or responses, and model correct responses. Provide a supportive, low-anxiety environment, avoid calling attention to grammar errors, and ask short *Wh-* questions.

**7. Keeping a frequently changing and updated Word Wall,** featuring current target words, which you and students refer to frequently throughout the day.

**8. Teaching learners how to study new words.** Help them learn how to create and organize their own dictionaries and flashcards, and then a procedure for studying these cards alone or with a partner. For example, have them:

1. Make the cards.
2. Select a group of cards.
3. Quiz themselves or partners on the cards.
4. Eliminate cards that have been mastered
5. Review all the known cards.
6. Select a new group of cards and repeat the process.

**9. Using many active, interactive strategies** to use and practice the vocabulary such as shared reading, shared writing, language experience, total physical response, chants, and I have– who has? (All are included in this book.).

**10. Providing active, interactive, cooperative games** for vocabulary practice, such as bingo, dominoes, jeopardy, "swat" the word, find the difference, concentration, or board games.

## Vocabulary-building Resources

The most common words in English: http://ef.com/english-resources/english-vocabulary/

Picturable word lists with pictures: http://simple.wikipedia.org/wiki/Wikipedia:Basic_English_picture_wordlist

Vocabulary Flashcards from ESL-kids.com: http://esl-kids.com/flashcards/flashcards.html

List of basic words: http://simple.wikipedia.org/wiki/Wikipedia:Basic_English_ordered_ wordlist

Simple English Wikipedia (written using basic words): https://simple.wikipedia.org/wiki/Main_Page

Flashcard practice: http://wikihow.com/Memorize-Flashcards-Effectively

Flashcard Games: http://eslkidstuff.com/flashcardgamescontent.htm#.VHIrKYvle-I

# DIPSTICKING: FREQUENTLY CHECKING COMPREHENSION OF EVERYONE IN THE CLASS

We need to include frequent pauses in our teaching to check the comprehension of all of our learners *during* our lessons. Below are

15 suggested ways for quickly *dipsticking*, or "checking the oil" of our classrooms (Levine & McCloskey, 2013; Saphier, Haley-Speca, & Gower, 2008).

- **Restating**. Ask students to restate your instructions and to demonstrate what they are to do.
- **Actions**. Ask students to answer a question by pointing, writing, marking–whatever is needed–so you can see that they truly understand.
- **Pair-Share**. Have students explain or restate something to a partner.
- **Nominations**. Don't call on hands; nominate students so that all have an equal chance to respond.
- **Clicker**. Use a computer clicker system to present questions and have all students respond.
- **Signals**. Have learners use signals such as thumbs up, thumbs down, a number of fingers, etc., so everyone can respond to a comprehension question at the same time.
- **Cards**. Have learners hold up one of a set of cards with numbers, letters, yes/no or true/false to show their answers to a question. They can also use color cards to show how well they understand:

    - ***Red*** = *Stop, I need help.*
    - ***Yellow*** = *I'm a little confused.*
    - ***Green*** = *Keep going, I understand.*

- **Slates**. Have students or pairs write answers on slates to respond. Computer notebooks can also be used as slates.
- **Language frames**. Use a language frame for learners to complete: *A continent south of North America is ____. Completed math papers go ____.*
- **Graphic organizers**. Have learners display concepts on Thinking Maps or other organizers.

- **Question formation**. Have learners write/ask a comprehension question.
- **Drawing**. Ask learners to draw a picture that shows understanding.
- **Games**. Play a game with questions/vocabulary from the lesson, such as I Have–Who Has?, Bingo, or Jeopardy and observe comprehension.
- **Summarizer**. Have students create a 3-2-1 Summary: 3 things you found out; 2 interesting things; 1 question you still have.
- **Exit/Entrance ticket**. Ask a review question to each student or request a short written response on a slip of paper as they enter or leave the classroom.

# PART II

# STRATEGIES FOR BUILDING COMPREHENSION

*Scaffolding* is a metaphor for the many ways we support learners to make it possible for them to do, with a little help, something they have not yet done independently. Many types of scaffolding provide support for learners of English as they acquire the skills of reading and learn to understand what they read. In this guide, we offer a variety of strategies for scaffolding at all stages of the reading process. Much of the scaffolding is not only about developing comprehension through reading, but also about using the language modes of listening, speaking, and writing about texts (Sadler, 2001).

*Before* learners read a text, we prepare them by activating their own experience and knowledge about the topic and issues of the text; by building background knowledge that might be unfamiliar and needed to understand the text; by teaching and previewing the structure of the text; and by pre-teaching some of the most important terms that may be new to learners.

*During* the reading, we provide scaffolding by developing learners' reading strategies; providing structures to support reading; glossing key terms; and directing them to use illustrations, context clues, and other keys to meaning.

*After* they read, we scaffold students' exploration of the meaning of a text through questions, discussions, and activities that help them expand their understanding.

The strategies provided for building comprehension before, during, and after reading a text include:

**12 Five Senses Chart**: Learners use their senses to describe and interpret descriptions.

**13 Anticipation Guide**: Learners answer questions to make predictions about their reading and check them with the text.

**14 Carousel**: Learners move around the room to share and discuss their projects.

**15 Creating Imagery**: Learners create and explore imagery in a text through visualization.

**16 Culture Map**: Learners explore cultural aspects of a text.

**17 Lineup**: Learners physically arrange themselves to show a sequence or evaluation.

**18 Making Inferences**: Learners use both information from the text and their own experience and knowledge to make inferences about what a text implies or might mean.

**19 Point of View/Character Chairs**: Learners take the point of view of characters in a narrative (fiction or nonfiction) while others ask them questions.

**20 Question-Answer-Relationship (QAR)**: Learners ask, answer, and learn to create key comprehension questions.

**21 Questioning the Author**: Learners explore the author's intentions and writing approach.

**22 Quickwrite**: Learners develop fluency and ideas by writing quickly without attending to form.

# 12

# FIVE SENSES CHART

A Five Senses chart is a graphic organizer that helps students discover and understand how an author refers to the senses in writing to make a text more vivid or real. Readers study a piece of writing—usually fiction or poetry—to find examples of the author's references to the five senses. Learners can also use a similar chart to plan their own figurative writing.

**Target Learning Strategies:** interpreting and using imagery; note taking; figurative writing

**Lesson Stages**: Through, Beyond

**Language Levels**: All

1. Ask learners to name the five senses. Read aloud examples of imagery from selected literature. Ask students to determine which sense the author refers to.
2. Choose a fiction selection or a poem rich with sensory imagery for learners to read.
3. Ask students read the piece and note examples where the author refers to the senses.
4. Have students reread the text closely to locate more places where the author refers to the senses. Ask them to quote the words the author used in the appropriate box in the graphic organizer.
5. In small groups, have readers take turns reading a quote, while others tell which sense is evoked.
6. Then have readers tell why they made the choices they did. **Example:** "This quote is about touch because you can feel the cold and hot food, and imagine what it might feel like to milk chickens."
7. Ask students to imagine what they are seeing, hearing, smelling, tasting, or touching through the images in the poem. Then they can record their ideas on a 5 senses chart like the one shown.

**Example**: "Childhood of the Ancients," by Andrew Hudgins [http://smiley963.tripod.com/poem7.html]

## Five Senses Chart: "Children of the Ancients" by Andrew Hudgins

| | |
|---|---|
| (eyes) | Pitch dark |
| (ear) | Plopped in front of you |
| (hand) | Cold sweet potato Hot food |
| (mouth) | Ice cream and soda pop |
| (nose) | Chicken fried pine straw |

# 13

# ANTICIPATION GUIDE

An Anticipation Guide is a way for learners to make predictions about a reading to activate learning and prepare for further study (Green, 1995). Before they read, students agree or disagree with statements about the text they will read. As they read, and after reading, learners check back to see how the text answers the questions and if their answers were correct.

**Target Learning Strategies:** making predictions; using an advanced organizer; distinguishing fact and opinion

**Lesson Stages:** Into, Through, Beyond

**Language Levels:** All

**Procedure:**

1. Prepare an anticipation guide by writing true/false statements about the text to be read. Use two basic types of statements: first, list the "big ideas" found in the text; second, state opinions or predictions about important supporting ideas, concepts, or events in the selection.

2. Before they read the selection, ask students to copy the chart and complete the "you" column of the Anticipation Guide individually by writing "T" if they think the statement is true or "F" if they think the statement is false. They should be ready to explain their answers.

3. Have learners work with a partner to share and compare their answers.

4. After reading the story, students respond to the statements again in the "text" column. This time they base their answers on information found in the text.

5. Student pairs discuss the answers, checking with the text to support answers.

6. Have learners discuss with the class the answers they changed and why.

**Example:** "My Korean Name," by Leonard Chang [http://leonardchang.tumblr.com/post/119702102307/my-korean-name]

| Anticipation Guide | | |
|---|---|---|
| Title & author: "My Korean Name," by Leonard Chang | | |
| You | Text | Statement |
| | | Chang had a problem with his grandfather. |
| | | Chang's grandfather liked to watch TV. |
| | | Chang understood Korean very well. |
| | | Chang learned what his name looked like in Korean. |
| | | Chang likes to think about his grandfather. |

# 14
## CAROUSEL

Carousel is an active, interactive summarizing or brainstorming activity in which learners share something they have learned and listen to and analyze what others have learned about a topic.

**Target Learning Strategies:** generating ideas; summarizing; listening; presenting; analyzing

**Lesson Stages:** Beyond: After reading (or writing, or as a theme-concluding activity)

**Language Levels:** All

**Procedure** (for Carousel as a summarizing activity for a theme or unit of study)**:**

**1.** Compose about eight summarizing questions. Write each on a piece of paper and post them on the wall of the classroom or the hallway.

**2.** Divide learners into eight groups.

**3.** Teach the roles for various group members and language they will need, for example:

- **Writer**: Writes down what group members say; asks questions to clarify. *Do you mean...?*

- **Leader**: Initiates discussion of each question, leading the group to analyze what has been written and asking for new ideas. *What can we add to the comments here?*

- **Reader**: Reads what has already been written on each new question; reads and summarizes information on the last question visited for the group. *Almost everyone agreed that...*

- **Includer**: Makes sure that everyone contributes to the discussion. *Tara, what do you think?*

**4.** Groups assign roles. Each group stands next to one question posted on the wall.

**5.** Groups take a few minutes to read, discuss, and write answers to the first question.

**6.** The teacher gives a signal, and groups rotate clockwise to the next question. There they read what has already been written, discuss what they have to add or comment on, and write it down.

**7.** Groups continue until they get to the last question. There, all the other members sit down, and the readers stay to share with the class what answers have been written to their last question.

**8.** Class and teacher can summarize and clarify answers as needed.

**Example:** Have learners answer summary questions about a topic they have studied; for example, *U.S. government.* Sample questions:

| Why do we need a bill of rights? What are the rights they guarantee? | What is one branch of the US government? What does it do? | Name an early president. When was he president? What happened then? | Use this frame to tell about a famous person. ____was born in____. ____died in____. He/she _____. (something important they did) |
|---|---|---|---|

# 15

# CREATING IMAGERY

Proficient readers create mental images as they process a text. They engage with the text and envision or respond to what they read by visualizing it. Creating this visual imagery requires inter-action with the text and deep and careful mental processing. This results in better recall and comprehension of the reading mate-rial (Buehl, 2008; Gambrell, Kapinus, & Wilson, 1987).

**Target Learning Strategies:** prediction; using imagery; using background knowledge

**Lesson Stages:** Into, Through

**Language Levels:** All

**Procedure:**

1. Identify a concept in a text for which visualization might improve readers' understanding, such as description, personification, characterization, or dialogue.
2. Read the text aloud and guide learners as they create mind pictures from the language.
3. Then have learners read the text and try to create their own mind pictures as they read. Optional: Learners can sketch images they come up with.
4. Ask learners to share their ideas in pairs or groups.
5. Have learners return to the text and compare the mental images of the concept with the text descriptions.

**Example:** Read aloud (or listen to the song) Bob Dylan's "Blowin' in the Wind" (lyrics available on Google Play Music). Then read short excerpts, for example, "How many times must a white dove sail before she sleeps in the sand?" Ask learners to create images (mind pictures) that are evoked by the poet's words and give them time for reflection. Have learners then describe those images to their partners. Finally, select students to share descriptions of their images with the class.

# 16

# CULTURE MAP

Culture frames our way of seeing and understanding the world around us. Literature-based lessons and activities give learners opportunities to think about culture and draw comparisons between other cultures and their own (Brisk & Harrington, 2007). Many unique cultural groups contribute to the fabric of the United States and have links to cultures around the world.

**Target Learning Strategies**: using what you know; classifying into meaningful groups

**Lesson Stages**: Into, Beyond

**Language Levels**: Intermediate

**Procedure:**

Choose a selection rich with rich cultural references. Make a culture map for focus with this selection, choosing elements of culture from the map below.

Help learners understand the meanings of the various cultural elements by having them find examples in their own cultures. The non-visible elements are, of course, the most difficult.

After students read the selection on their own, have them look for the cultural elements on the culture map.

In small groups, they note and compare the cultural elements identified and find the best examples.

Students write the examples in the column on the right. Not all stories will provide examples of all elements, and students may identify other cultural elements not listed on the chart.

| Culture Map | | |
|---|---|---|
| **Title of Selection** | **Author** | |
| | **Culture Elements in Text** | **Page Number** |
| *Visable culture elements*, e.g., food, music, events, holidays, names, clothing, occupations | | |
| *How people in the culture see the worlds*, e.g., religion, values, attitudes about others, health practices | | |
| *Communication:* Language, greetings, communication styles, non-verbal communication | | |

**Example:** Before they read the West African Folk Tale "Why Anansi Has Eight Thin Legs," by Gary Soto [http://africa.mrdonn.org/anansi.html], have learners complete a culture map about food and food traditions in their homes. After reading, they can create maps from the cultures revealed in the story to compare with their own and peers' maps.

# 17

## LINEUP

Lineups are an engaging way to have learners practice oral language (Levine & McCloskey, 2013). As students mingle and move around, they ask and answer questions and compare their responses about a topic. Eventually, they find their position according to some criterion that can be ordered. The line-up can be used as a quick warm up, a review of a topic, for dividing students into pairs or groups by matching those standing next to each other, etc.

**Target Learning Strategies:** cooperative learning; comprehension; fluency; critical thinking

**Lesson Stages:** Into, Through, Beyond

**Language Levels:** All

**Procedure:**

Ask a question that results in answers that can be ordered, for example:

- *What time do you get to school in the morning?*
- *How far do you travel to school?*
- *What is the month and day of your birthday?*
- *What is your favorite number?*
- *(What is your) height?*
- *What is your shoe size?*
- *How many brothers and sisters do you have?*
- *What time did you go to bed last night?*
- *How many marbles do you think are in the jar?*

1. Model and practice asking and answering the question so everyone has the language they need.
2. Ask students to interact with one another, sharing information about the question in order to identify their place in line, for example, from the earliest to the latest morning risers.

3. Students use the questions and answers to line up in the correct order.
4. Ask students to share their responses with the whole class (for example, *I got up at 6:25 this morning*) to check if they have positioned themselves correctly in the line.
5. Conclude the activity, or…
6. "Fold" the line in half (last person pairs with first, etc.) to create partners for the next activity.

**Example:** When studying about students' (or their family members') journeys from one country to another, have learners research and compute the distance of the trip and then ask one another about the distance in order to line up according to the distance they traveled.

# 18

# MAKING INFERENCES

Proficient readers are able to actively interact with a text, link their own knowledge and experience with information in the text, and make inferences about possible implied messages in the text (Gallagher, 2004). "Reading between the lines" means learners can infer ideas about characters, places, writer's views, etc. This graphic organizer scaffolds inference-making and allows learners to identify meanings that are perhaps implied but not stated in the text.

| Making Inferences | | |
|---|---|---|
| Context clue | My experience & knowledge | My inference |
| | | |
| | | |

**Target Learning Strategies**: deduction; elaboration; making inferences

**Lesson Stage**: Beyond

**Language Levels**: Low-Intermediate to Advanced

**Procedure**:

1. After reading a text or studying a topic, introduce the graphic organizer below. Explain that making inferences is what detectives do. To illustrate, use a well-known experience familiar to your students. For example, if they see the sign *No cell phones*, what does their experience or background knowledge tell them? (That there is a reason cell phones cannot be used–perhaps a performance, or a concern that cell phones will interfere with other electronics, or with learning, etc.). Explain that inference involves combining words and clues in the text, related understandings, and our experience.

2. Select context clues/facts from a text. Include ones that students might be confused about. Guide them to write down a clue or fact from the text (about characters, setting, communication, etc.). Select the first few clues to get learners started. Then have them write what they know about the fact in the second column. Last, encourage students to make a conclusion combining the fact/clue and their knowledge.

3. Complete the chart including four or five clues or events. Have students share their inferences in groups or in front of the class.

**Example**: As you study a graphic about refugees (e.g., [http://therefugeeproject.org/]) help learners find questions and collect clues to make inferences about refugee patterns.

| Making Inferences | | |
|---|---|---|
| Where have most immigrants come from? | | |
| What states/counties have the most African immigrants? | | |
| How do you expect this map to change by 2050? | | |

# 19

# POINT OF VIEW / CHARACTER CHAIRS

In this cooperative learning strategy, learners take on the roles of characters from a story and work to understand the motivation behind the actions of these characters (Zwier, 2004). Groups of learners write questions to an assigned character from the story. Learners from each group come to the front of the class to answer the questions, as if they were the characters. This strategy guides learners to re-read a passage in order to ask and answer questions, understand and identify with characters, practice speaking in the first person, and have fun.

**Target Learning Strategies**: cooperation; prediction; questioning for clarification

**Lesson Stages**: Beyond

**Language Levels**: Advanced

**Procedure**:

1. After learners have read a fiction or nonfiction selection with strong characters, have them work in groups of about four to think of questions to ask a character.
2. Assign each group one character. Include one non-human living thing or something inanimate—for example, if you were reading the story of Rosa Parks (US Civil Rights heroine of the Montgomery Boycott), you might choose the bus. If you were reading about Wangari Maathai (environmental heroine from Kenya) you might include a tree.
3. Model forming and asking questions and, if needed, provide question prompts like *Who____? What____? When____? Where ____? Why_____? How____?* Encourage learners to ask more questions that start with *Why* and *How*—questions that don't have one-word answers.
4. Ask each group to write three or more questions to their assigned character, for example, *Bus driver, why did you ask*

*Rosa to leave her seat?* Encourage students to return to the
text to look for good questions.

5. When learners are ready, have each group send one
   person to the front of the class to play the part of their
   character. You can label the chairs with names of the
   characters or put signs around the necks of characters to
   show who they are.
6. Invite the class to ask characters questions. You will
   probably start with questions from that character's
   group, but can soon open up the questioning to
   everyone. Remind the questioners to tell which character
   they are addressing the question to.
7. The characters answer the question as completely as
   possible, staying in character.

**Example:** After studying the Montgomery bus boycott, students
write questions for Rosa Parks, the bus driver, the bus, a white
passenger, a black passenger, and a police officer. Students take
turns taking the parts, sitting in labeled chairs before the class.
The class asks the characters questions, and the role-players
answer in character. Repeat with new students playing the roles.

# 20

# QUESTION-ANSWER RELATIONSHIP (QAR)

The Question-Answer Relationship (QAR) strategy (Raphael,

1986) identifies four types of questions that students learn to ask and answer:

1. "Right There" questions (the answer is clearly stated in one place in the selection);
2. "Think and Search" questions (the answer requires students to look for the answer in more than one part of the story);
3. "Author and You" questions (the answer is a combination of information from what the author wrote and what the reader knows); and
4. "On your Own" questions (the answer comes from the reader's background knowledge and experience, in interaction with the ideas from the story).

These questions ask students to think about a text at four different levels, and enhance both comprehension and thinking skills.

**Target Learning Strategies:** reviewing; retelling; negotiation of meaning

**Lesson Stages:** Through, Beyond

**Language Levels:** All

**Procedure:**

1. Explain and model the four levels of questions to students: *Right There, Think and Search, Author and You,* and *On Your Own.*
2. Prepare a list of questions in the four areas for the students to answer based on a selection from the text.
3. In small groups of 3-4, have students read/watch a selection and answer the questions. They indicate the

QAR category for each question and justify their decisions.

4. Ask students to read/watch another selection and write their own QAR questions. Each group exchanges their questions with another group, answers them, and categorizes them into QAR levels.

**Example:** QAR questions can be used with any reading, viewing, or listening activity. After students become familiar with these types of questions, encourage them to begin developing the questions themselves and asking them of one another. Sample questions for the video, "Monarch Butterfly Amazing Migration": https://youtu.be/LawHWsIqa5s or the wordless story of the Monarch: https://youtu.be/yIFB9reAkwU

*Right There*: Where does a butterfly lay its eggs? Why?

*Think and Search*: Why do monarchs have to migrate?

*Author and Me*: What do I think the writer/director's purpose is in making this video?

*On My Own*: What do I think people could do to help the monarchs?

# 21

## QUESTIONING THE AUTHOR

This comprehension checking strategy encourages students to think beyond the written text. It guides them to think about the author's intentions in writing the text, the message of the text, and the author's ability to communicate the message clearly to the audience. Students answer and discuss five basic questions about a text that help them to better construct its meaning (Van De Weghe, 2007; McKeown, Beck, & Worthy, 1993).

**Target learning strategies:** inferring; summarizing; synthesizing; reviewing

**Lesson Stages:** Through, Beyond

**Language Levels:** All

**Procedure:**

**1.** Review the text and identify parts that could cause problems for students to understand.

**2.** Have students read a section you have selected.

**3.** Guide students to discuss the selected part by asking the following questions:

1. What is the author trying to tell you?
2. Why is the author telling you that?
3. Is the message said clearly?
4. How might the author have written it more clearly?
5. What might you have wanted to say instead?

**4.** As students address the questions, they share their ideas with one another and construct the meaning of the text.

**5.** Encourage students to use the questions independently when they read a challenging text.

**Example:** Guide students to use the strategy as they read the poem "Knoxville, Tennessee" by Nikki Giovanni [https://www.poets.org/poetsorg/poem/knoxville-tennessee] for a second time. Have them share and discuss their ideas addressing the following questions (or, if you wish, use all five questions).

1. What is the author trying to say about being a young girl in Knoxville, Tennessee?
2. Why does the author talk about specific foods?

# 22

# QUICKWRITE

Quickwrite (Fisher & Frey, 2008) is a strategy teachers use to help
students generate ideas by writing quickly about a topic. This

process helps students explore and activate background knowledge. Often students don't know what they want to say when they begin writing–it is the process of writing that makes their thinking clear. After writing, students share their ideas and listen to what others have written, thereby clarifying their own thoughts and gaining new ideas and insights.

**Target Learning Strategies:** activating prior knowledge; active listening; organizing for writing

**Lesson Stages:** Into, Through, Beyond

**Language Levels:** All

**Procedure:**

1. Ask students to write for about 5 minutes without stopping about a topic related to a text they are going to read.
2. Tell learners that if they don't know what to write, they should write the last word they wrote over and over until new ideas come into their heads. Tell them not to worry now about form or spelling–the important thing for a quickwrite is just to get ideas down on paper.
3. After the five minutes of writing, have students find partners and take turns sharing what they wrote with each other.
4. Partners then ask questions and offer comments and encouragement about one another's writing.
5. Ask for volunteers to read from what they wrote to the class.
6. Use learners' ideas as pre-assessment to guide introduction of topics. Refer back to their original ideas as appropriate.

**Example**: "Gate A-4," [https://poets.org/poetsorg/poem/gate-4] is a selection in which Naomi Shihab Nye reflects on an experience in an airport. Before reading the poem, have learners reflect on the experience of travel–is there anything that makes them anxious or worried? Have they ever seen a stranger in trouble? Has a stranger ever been kind to them? Then have learners follow the procedure above to write and share quickwrites on their topics. After the reading, learners can reflect and compare/contrast their own travel experiences with that of the author.

# PART III

# READING PROCESS STRATEGIES

Reading presents many challenges to learners of English: students may struggle hearing or producing the sounds of the language; they may not know the vocabulary or the grammar. Some students bring high levels of literacy from their first language; some do not. Some students speak languages with grammar and vocabulary and alphabet that are closely related to English; some have different alphabets, few similarities in grammar, and few cognates.

In this section, we include a variety of processes for providing scaffolding to learners as they read texts. The strategies also integrate the other language modes of speaking, reading, and writing. These strategies enable teachers to provide different types and levels of support (oral or written), depending on the genre and difficulty of the text, and on the reading and language levels of the learners.

These strategies also motivate learners in different ways: with a variety of active roles in reading, opportunities to focus on different aspects of the text during different readings, and alternative ways to read texts that may better suit students with different learning styles and preferences. These strategies include the following ways of reading, each of which is described on the pages that follow:

**23. Choral Reading**: Students read a text together in unison or in groups.

**24. Independent Reading**: Students, with scaffolding, read on their own.

**25. Jigsaw Reading**: Students divide the reading into parts and teach one another.

**26. Paired Reading**: Students use a variety of structures to read with partners.

**27. Teacher Read Aloud**: Teachers use effective ways to read aloud to students.

**28. Reader's Theater**: Teacher and/or students convert a narrative text to a dialogue and read the text as a play, often with a narrator.

**29. Reciprocal Teaching**: Students exchange roles as "teacher" and "student," reading short segments of text to one another and learning to ask and answer questions key to comprehension.

# 23

# CHORAL READING

Choral reading is reading aloud in unison with the class. After hearing the teacher read and discussing the selection, learners reread the text together. This strategy improves learners' fluency and allows them to participate actively in the reading activity, without self-consciousness about their performance (Rasinski, 2010). This is especially effective with pieces designed to be presented orally, such as speeches, plays, and poetry.

**Target Learning Strategies:** reading fluently; reading accurately; developing the sounds, rhythm and stress patterns of English; confidence development; enjoyment of literature

**Lesson Stages:** Into, Through, Beyond

**Language Levels:** All

**Procedure:**

After reading a selection aloud, invite the class to read along with you.

**Possible Variations:**

- **Student leader.** Have a student lead the choral reading while you stand at the back and listen to various readers, noting issues for future instruction.
- **Antiphonal Reading**. Divide students into groups to read different parts of the text.
- **Dialogue**. Assign narrator and parts of a play or dialogue to groups instead of individuals.
- **Cumulative**. Gradually add more readers as the piece continues
- **Impromptu.** Students join in and fade out as they choose during choral reading. They might choose to emphasize certain words or sections of the text or read alternate lines. They choose ahead of time what sections of the text they will read.

**Example:** While reading the poem, "Where I'm From," by Georgia Ella Lyon [http://georgeellalyon.com/where.html], the class uses several variations of choral reading to read the text together. They read all together; they read alternate stanzas; different individuals read the poem a couplet at a time, and students read stanzas individually while everyone reads the words "I am from."

# 24

# INDEPENDENT READING

This strategy builds students' reading fluency and independence as readers. Students are given a reading assignment at the appropriate level of language proficiency. After an introduction and an activity or questions to focus reading, they read on their own. Teachers can read their own materials as students read, or discuss and guide reading with individual students or small groups.

**Target Learning Strategies:** autonomy; reading fluency; self-comprehension checking

**Lesson Stages:** Through

**Language Levels:** All

**Procedure:**

1. Introduce a reading text that is at a level that students can read independently.
2. Provide an introduction and overview; make connections between the reading and what learners already know; build background; and introduce key words that might interfere with comprehension.
3. Offer an activity or questions to focus the purpose of reading.
4. Remind students of one or more strategies they have learned to use when reading independently, for example: prediction, creating imagery, guessing meaning of unknown words from context, or using visuals.
5. Provide time for the reading or assign it to be read at home.
6. Monitor frequently to assure that students are reading successfully. Provide support when they struggle with the text.

**Example:** Using the selection "Are We Having Fun Yet?" by Ryan Levy [http://merlynspen.org/stuff/contentmgr/files/9cd4303980bad 4e840694c7a761c08e3/read/10.3.es.1.pdf], have learners first make predictions about the text, then read the essay on their own and at their own pace. After reading, they can check and expand their comprehension of the text.

# 25

# JIGSAW READING

In jigsaw reading (Aaronson, http://jigsaw.org/), learners become experts on one portion of a reading and share their expertise with others. This is a way for learners to study a longer text without having to read every part. Because English learners read slowly as they learn, this strategy can expose them to longer, important texts. Learners share summaries of their texts and hear about the rest from peers. Everyone shares responsibility for learning.

**Target learning strategies:** summarizing; analyzing; making inferences

**Lesson Stages:** Through and Beyond

**Language Levels**: All

**Procedure**:

1. Divide a reading into smaller sections.
2. Divide participants into "home groups" of about 4 (or the number of sections of the reading).
3. In the home groups, assign each student a different "expert" number (e.g., for sections 1, 2, 3, or 4).
4. Students then reassemble into "expert groups" according to their numbers.
5. Expert groups meet to read and study their assigned section, and plan how to teach about it to their home groups. You may direct them to create a graphic organizer or other summarizing tool.
6. Experts return to their home groups, where each expert, in the sequence of the reading, summarizes and teaches about the section they read.
7. The teacher may have groups submit a summary to demonstrate their understanding or complete another comprehension check.

**Example:** Use the jigsaw strategy to have learners read a selection from a newspaper or textbook, or an article on the Internet,

for example, "How to Study for a Test"
[http://wikihow.com/Study-for-a-Test]. Divide students into
groups of about 5. Each group member reads 1 page (or 1
section) of the selection, meets with the expert group to discuss,
and then returns to the home group to summarize.

# 26
# PAIRED READING

Paired reading or buddy reading is a cooperative strategy that research indicates has produced significant gains in comprehension and fluency (Calderón, 2007; Samway, 1995; Topping, 1995). When using this strategy, students interact with a text multiple times in a variety of ways.

**Target Learning Strategies**: reviewing; retelling; summarizing; negotiation of meaning

**Lesson Stages**: Into, Through, Beyond

**Language Levels**: All

**Procedure**:

1. Introduce the students to the paired reading strategy. Begin by establishing a routine for students to adopt so that they know the step-by-step requirements for engaging in paired reading. Begin with one variation and use it a few times before introducing another variation: Will they read out loud, simultaneously? Will they take turns, with each person reading a paragraph? a page?

2. Give students guiding questions to focus their reading attention.

3. Ask them to first read a new or review selection silently; then read aloud to their partners.

4. Depending on your goals, you might pair more fluent readers with less fluent readers, same level readers, or have students self-select their reading partners. Students can take turns reading by sentence, paragraph, page or chapter.

5. Tell them what error-correction procedure to use when supporting their partner's reading. Model the procedure to ensure that students understand how to use the strategy. For example: a) ignore errors that don't affect meaning, b) give a nonverbal signal if a word is misread, or c) say the word correctly immediately after the error.

**Possible Variations**:

- **Echo Reading**: One partner reads a line. The other partner repeats the line.
- **Expressive Reading**: One partner reads a chunk of text. The other reads the chunk with expression.
- **Part Reading**: One partner reads all the characters' parts, using a different voice for each. The other partner reads the narrator's parts.
- **Taking Turns**: One partner reads a sentence, paragraph, or page. The other partner summarizes. Then they exchange roles.
- **Silent Reading**: Partners read silently, sitting near one another so that they can ask each other for help when they need it.
- **Learners Read Aloud to a Parent or Sibling**: Re-read something from school to parents at home. Summarize in the home language if it is different from English.

**Example:** Learners might use paired reading to study the history of US food guides: [http://choosemyplate.gov/food-groups/downloads/myplate/abriefhistoryofusdafoodguides.pdf]. Partners take turns reading and listening, a section at a time. After each section, the listener shares the main ideas. Partners take turns reading and listening, a paragraph at a time. After each paragraph, the listener summarizes the main ideas of the paragraph.

# 27

# TEACHER READ ALOUD

Good readers are often learners who have been read to (Trelease, 2006). Reading aloud to learners allows them to experience texts that they are not yet able to read on their own, and provides an opportunity for you to share your enthusiasm about reading and books, and to model the patterns and rhythms of English.

**Target Learning Strategies:** developing reading comprehension; retelling; summarizing; negotiation of meaning

**Lesson Stages:** Into, Through, Beyond

**Language Levels:** All

**Procedure:**

1. Plan to read aloud frequently and regularly to your class
2. Work to read aloud clearly, with expressiveness, varying pitch, volume, and pace to provide drama and create interest. Don't read too quickly–give your English learners time to process what they hear.
3. Select high-interest texts that you like and that you think your students will enjoy. Work to include texts about/from students' home cultures.
4. Introduce books carefully, building background and helping learners make connections between their own experiences and the literature.
5. Stop occasionally to check comprehension and provide clarification of difficult concepts and language. You might occasionally ask a learner to summarize what you have read to check comprehension.
6. When learners are ready, move on to chapter books, reading a section each day. Start with a little review of what has happened before, and then continue the story.

**Possible Variations:**

- **Deep reading**: Focus on one author/subject for a while–have students become "experts."

- **Conversational activities and projects**: Learners need to "chew and digest" what they've read. Encourage them to talk about the books and work with the texts, using many of the strategies for working with literature in this guide.
- **Audiobooks**: Have learners listen to audiobooks, either the authors' own interpretation of the text or that of professional actors. They may like to read along as they listen to the text.
- **Silent reading**: Partners read silently, sitting near one another so that they can ask each other for help when they need it.

**Example**: With older students: Read aloud the poem "Supple Cord," by Naomi Shihab Nye [http://poetryfoundation.org/poems-and-poets/poems/detail/49444], and discuss the ideas of the poem before the learners go on to use paired reading to share and explore the work.

# 28

# READER'S THEATER

In reader's theater, learners read plays out loud, taking the parts
of characters and the narrator. The activity is fun for learners,

yet it demands good comprehension of the text to read expressively, and good oral language to provide an interesting and easily understandable performance. Worthy and Prater (2002) suggest that the goal of reader's theater is to give students motivation to read and reread scripts, thus improving both reading fluency and reading comprehension. Expressive reading also enhances comprehension.

**Target Learning Strategies:** predicting; questioning; clarifying; summarizing

**Lesson Stages:** Into, Through, Beyond

**Language Levels:** Advanced beginner to advanced

**Procedure:**

1. Introduce Reader's Theater with a prepared script. Create your own from a text with lots of dialogue, or locate a prepared script. (See a large collection of excellent scripts at http://thebestclass.org/rtscripts.html.)
2. Adjust the assignment of characters to match students' reading levels.
3. Have learners read the script aloud, taking the parts of various characters.
4. Help learners revise and perfect their reading.
5. Students perform the skit by reading it aloud in character, with a few minimal props (such as hats) to suggest scenes and characters.
6. Later, involve students in creating their own scripts from texts with lots of dialogue.

**Example:** Have learners use Readers' Theater to read excerpts from *The Diary of Anne Frank* [http://www.rhetorik.ch/Aktuell/16/02_13/frank_diary.pdf]. If there aren't enough roles for the class in your selection, several students can read the lines of one character, or take turns for different readings. To help learners know which are their parts to read, have them mark the text one of these ways:

- Rewrite the story as a script with characters' names showing their parts and make copies.
- Highlight each character's part on that copy of the script.
- If learners have copies they can write on, have them mark their own parts in pencil.
- Use sticky notes to mark a character's lines in a text they cannot write in.

**Options**: Many reader's theater scripts are available on the Internet. An excellent place to start is: [http://teachingheart.net/readerstheater.htm].

# 29

# RECIPROCAL TEACHING

Reciprocal teaching (Palencsar & Brown, 1986) teaches learners to focus intently on understanding and remembering what they read by using four key strategies: predicting, questioning, clarifying, and summarizing. Palencsar & Brown (1986) and Ozcus (2003) found significant improvement in reading comprehension from use of this strategy.

**Target Learning Strategies:** predicting; questioning; clarifying; summarizing

**Lesson Stages:** Into, Through, Beyond

**Language Levels:** Advanced Beginner to Advanced

**Procedure:**

**1.** Begin by introducing the four reading strategies of Reciprocal Teaching. Teach, demonstrate, and have learners practice them one at a time over several days or longer.

- **Predicting.** Prediction is used in the **Into** and **Through** stages to make logical guesses about what will come next in the story. Language used: *I think...*, *I bet...*, *I predict...*, *I suppose*, *I imagine...*, *I wonder if...*
- **Questioning.** Effective readers ask themselves a variety of questions during the **Through** stage of a reading lesson: questions about the main idea, important details, and textual inferences gathered as students read. Language used: questions with *who, what, when, where, why*, and so on.
- **Clarifying.** During the **Through** stage, while students are reading, they learn to use clarifying strategies such as rereading, looking at word parts, looking at the context, thinking about similar words, and trying another word that makes sense. Language used: *This is not clear; I can't figure out...*; or *This word is tricky because....*
- **Summarizing.** Used while reading in the **Through** stage and to review reading during the **Beyond** stage,

summarizing uses many skills and strategies at one time to remember and rearrange the most important information in a text. Language used: *The most important ideas were*; *First..., next..., then...finally.*

**2.** Small groups of 2-5 can use reciprocal teaching. One student assumes the role of leader. The leader reads a paragraph aloud, while the rest of the group reads silently.

**3.** The leader asks the group to use the four comprehension strategies: predicting what will happen next, answering questions about the story, clarifying words or details, and summarizing the paragraph.

**4.** The next student in the group then becomes the leader for the next section or paragraph, and so on until the whole reading selection is completed.

**Example:** Assign partners to read a mathematics word problem using reciprocal teaching. Word problem examples: [http://math.about.com/od/1/]

# 30

# WORD SPLASH

Word Splash (Saphier, Haley-Speca, & Gower, 2008) is an

activity that activates learning about a topic. Learners are challenged to discover relationships among important words in a text.

**Target Learning Strategies:** vocabulary study; classification; making connections

**Lesson Stage:** Intro

**Language Levels:** All

**Procedure:**

1. Choose key words from a text that learners will read.
2. On a chart, transparency, or board, "splash the words" in a random design.
3. Invite learners to study the words using a glossary, dictionary, and teacher explanation as necessary.
4. Then, challenge learners to make connections between the words by using sentences to predict what the reading will be about.
5. The same word splash can be used as assessment at the end of the lesson–ask learners to write sentences that connect the words and that use them correctly to tell about the reading.

**Example:** This Word Splash is used with Sharon Creech's poem, "Fears and Loves" from her book, *Heartbeat* [http://archive.today/Z4lD1]. After explaining the vocabulary and having learners demonstrate understanding, task them to connect two of the words in the Word Splash in a sentence that shows the meaning of both words.

# PART IV

# GRAPHIC ORGANIZERS FOR TEXT STRUCTURE

Graphic organizers are tools that can help to level the playing field for English learners by recognizing and enhancing their cognitive abilities. By using pictures and designs to organize texts and to illustrate principles, students are able to use visual cues that reveal structure and meaning, and enhancements to context that support comprehension of content.

**Before** reading, a graphic organizer can be used as a map of the organization of a text. Captions for the graphic can introduce key language of the reading in small chunks accompanied by pictures or graphics that provide clues to their meaning.

**During** reading, graphic organizers aligned to the organization of a text (for example, a Venn diagram for a compare-contrast essay) can help learners take notes and build comprehension.

**After** reading, graphic organizers can be used to analyze and/or summarize a reading, as well as to outline a piece of writing.

At all stages of reading, graphic organizers can provide English learners with multimodal exposure to text and help to clarify the structures of both the language and the content. The following eight graphic organizers are described, with examples, in this section:

**30. Cause and Effect**: Learners explore relationships when one thing leads to another.

**31. Compare/Contrast Graphic Organizer: Venn Diagram**: Learners compare and contrast two things or concepts, showing what is the same and what is different.

**32. Continuity Scale**: Learners evaluate things or ideas by organizing them on a scale from smaller to larger.

**33. Narrative Structure–Story Map**: Learners map the sequence of the common organization of a story.

**34. Narrative Structure–Reporter's Outline**: Learners answer the questions a reporter asks when developing a story.

**35. Persuasive Essay Sandwich**: Learners use a sandwich metaphor to take apart or put together the elements of persuasive writing.

**36. Problem/Solution Chart**: Learners focus on problems described and attempts to solve them in either a fiction or nonfiction text.

**37. T-List/Table/Matrix**: Students use simple matrices to organize ideas or data.

**38. Time Sequence–Showing Chronology**: Learners explore texts by time sequence.

# 31

# CAUSE AND EFFECT GRAPHIC ORGANIZER

An essential comprehension element for English learners is understanding how one event can lead to another (Zwier, 2004).

Cause and effect graphic organizers can help readers see the relationship between something that happens to the events that led up to that occurrence. Learners can use these organizers as note-taking aids to improve comprehension when reading texts, as preparation for discussion or texts, and also as pre-writing aids.

**Target Learning Strategies**: directed attention; reviewing key ideas and details; understanding cause/effect relationships

**Lesson Stages**: Through, Beyond

**Language Levels**: All

**Procedure**:

1. Model the process with an example from a previous reading/viewing.
2. Select a cause-effect relationship sequence in the selection.
3. Next, discuss with students the relationship between the causes and the effect.
4. Write the causes and effects in the appropriate columns.
5. Help learners make a concluding statement about the cause and effect and write it in a box across the bottom.
6. When students understand the process, have them work in small groups or as individuals to make cause-effect charts of their own about readings or to prepare for writing.

**Example:** After reading an online biography, for example, of Nelson Mandela [http://ducksters.com/biography/nelson_mandela.php], have students create a graphic organizer of the causes and effects of how the person came to be well known.

| Cause and Effect | | | |
|---|---|---|---|
| **Life event** | **Cause** | | **Effect** |
| Mandela was born during apartheid. | White leaders segregated the society and gave whites many privileges over non-whites. | ⟶ | Mandela became an activist against apartheid. |
| Mandela led the African National Congress. | | ⟶ | |
| Mandela went to prison for 27 years. | | ⟶ | |
| Mandela became president of South Africa. | | ⟶ | |
| Mandela won the Nobel Peace Prize. | | ⟶ | |

# 32

# COMPARE/CONTRAST GRAPHIC ORGANIZER: VENN DIAGRAM

The Venn diagram is a graphic organizer that charts comparisons and contrasts or similarities and differences between two or more concepts, sets, or terms. John Venn (1880) first used these diagrams to illustrate formal logic assumptions. In language teaching, Venn diagrams can be used to compare and contrast words or ideas to classify information into categories, visualize relationships among words or ideas, focus attention on key information, and record similarities and differences.

**Target Learning Strategies**: analyzing text structure; comparing and contrasting elements

**Lesson Stages**: Into, Through, Beyond

**Language Levels**: All

**Procedure**:

1. Demonstrate the use of a Venn diagram. First, draw a blank Venn diagram on the board.
2. Label the two sides with two contrasting things, for example, two class members, and label the center "both."
3. Help learners describe the two people and decide which descriptions are about one, which are about the other, and which are about both.
4. Write these descriptions in the correct portion of the diagram. Use these descriptions with language frames (Strategy #5, p. 16) to compose compare/contrast statements about the two people.
5. Explain that these can be used as well in describing things we read and write about.

**Example:** Ötzi is the frozen mummy found in the Alps of a man who lived over 3000 years ago. After reading or viewing a selection from the Internet about Ötzi [e.g., https://en.wikipedia.org/wiki/Otzi], have learners use a Venn diagram to compare the life of this prehistoric human with their own lives. Have learners use the Venn diagram to speak or write comparative sentences about Ōtzi.

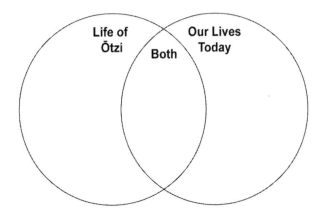

# 33

# CONTINUITY SCALE GRAPHIC ORGANIZER

Graphic organizers help learners to "transform information into knowledge" (Hyerle & Hyerle, 2009). Continuity scale graphic organizers assist higher-order learning by showing learners how to put items in order along a scale. Like other graphic organizers, they provide learners with a visual tool for better comprehension of the text and organization of ideas before, during, or after a text.

**Target Learning Strategies**: grouping; note taking; evaluating; using physical actions to remember concepts or information

**Lesson Stages**: Into, Through, Beyond

**Language Levels**: All

**Procedure**:

1. Provide students with a copy of a continuity scale graphic organizer with points along a scale, like one of those below. Draw it on the board for them to copy.
2. Show students how events or information can be placed on the scale from left to right or right to left according to given criteria (e.g., time, importance, interest, quality). Write an example on the board to model what they will do later, for example, the sequence of events in a day or important dates in one's life.
3. Ask students, as they read or review a text, to place events or information along the continuum according to the criteria.
4. After they finish reading, students can compare and defend their findings with a partner or as a whole class.

———|———|———|———|———|———|———

**first event**                                                    **last event**

———|———|———|———|———|———|———

**most important**                                          **least important**

———|———|———|———|———|———|———

**most helpful**                                          **most embarrassing**

**Example:** Have students read about an important issue, for example, How to keep water clean [https://tvakids.com/environment/cleanwater.htm] Create heading strips of the main ideas, such as "Help clean up streams." After reading the selection and studying the topic, students put heading strips along two continua: *not important – important* and *easy to do – hard to do*. They then use these to write about an action they might take.

# 34

# NARRATIVE GRAPHIC ORGANIZER: STORY MAP

A story map outlines the structure of narrative fiction or nonfiction and includes the basic story elements of character, setting, goal, events, and resolution.

**Target Learning Strategies:** summarizing and analyzing narrative text structure; outlining a narrative

**Lesson Stages:** Into, Through, Beyond

**Language Levels:** All

**Procedure:**

1. Model making a story map with a familiar narrative, such as a fairy tale or folk tale, or a recent event in school, pointing out the elements of the story.
2. Scaffold creating a story map with students the first time.
3. Then have students create a blank map and fill it in as they read a narrative.
4. Later, students can use the map to outline their own stories.

**Example:** This example uses a shortened version of the story of Aladdin, from *Tales of the Arabian Nights* [http://shortstoriesshort.com/story/aladdin/]. In this example, learners have outlined main events of the traditional tale.

| Story Map For "Aladdin," from The Arabian Nights | |
| --- | --- |
| **Characters:** | **Setting:** |
| Aladdin<br>Aladdin's mother<br>Sorcerer<br>Genie<br>Princess Badroulbadour<br>Sorcerer's brother | San Francisco |

**Events** (things that happened):

*First:* Sorcerer tricks Aladdin to go to get a magical oil lamp from a magic cave.

Next:  Aladdin is trapped in the cave, finds a way to use a magic ring to make a genie (or jinni) appear and release him from the cave.

Next:  Aladdin takes the lamp home. When his mother tries to clean it, another genie appears to do whatever they ask.

Next:  Aladdin becomes rich and marries Princess Badroulbadour.

Next:  The sorcerer comes back, tricks Aladdin's wife into giving him the lamp, and takes everything he owns.

Next:  Aladdin uses the magic of the ring, along with the wisdom and help of his wife, to recover the lamp.

Next:  The sorcerer's brother tries to destroy Aladdin by tricking his wife again. The genie warns Aladdin of the danger, and slays the imposter.

**Resolution:** (how the problem is solved)

Aladdin successfully destroys the sorcerer and his brother. Everyone lives happily ever after, and Aladdin eventually becomes the Sultan.

**Moral:** It pays to be good, kind, and clever.

**Variation:** In the next chapter, a Reporter's Outline (or Sunshine Outline) is used to outline the facts in a narrative story and a narrative essay.

# 35

# NARRATIVE GRAPHIC ORGANIZER: REPORTER'S OUTLINE

A reporter's outline (or sunshine outline) is another type of narrative graphic organizer designed to organize the facts about an event.

**Example 1:** Students have outlined the basic facts and events of the children's classic "The Three Bears."

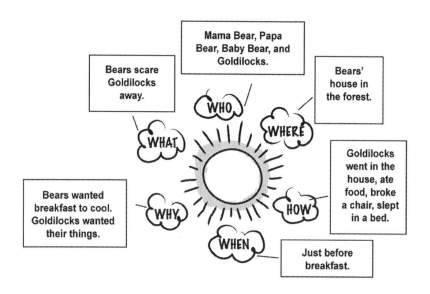

**Example 2**: Reporter's Outline for "Are We Having Fun Yet?" by Ryan Levy.

[http://www.merlynspen.org/contentmgr/showdetails.php/id/29139/search/true]

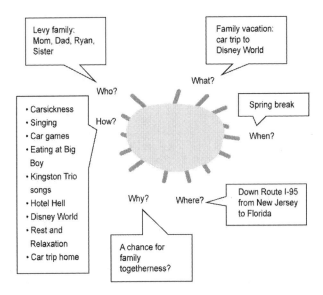

# 36

# PERSUASIVE ESSAY SANDWICH

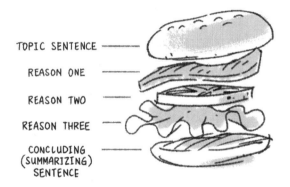

TOPIC SENTENCE

REASON ONE

REASON TWO

REASON THREE

CONCLUDING
(SUMMARIZING)
SENTENCE

Nearly every culture has a food in which ingredients are held together with some kind of bread to make a hand-held meal. This graphic organizer uses the sandwich as a metaphor to help learners see how a persuasive paragraph is organized.

**Target Learning Strategies**: planning; organizing; directed attention; summarizing

**Lesson Stages**: Beyond

**Language Levels**: Intermediate to Advanced

**Procedure**:

**1.** Use this organizer after reading a text that brings up issues students feel strongly about, such as a speech or story that has more than one point of view.

A. First, think about what perspective your argument will take. Perhaps that people should take better care of their streets by picking up the trash in front of their home.

B. Then, list reasons why this is a good arrangement, i.e.:

   i. The streets will be safer, preventing people from falling.
   ii. People will be healthier.
   iii. It is easier to keep things clean if every person does his/her part.
   iv. The streets will look more beautiful if they are clean.

C. Then, organize your argument with a topic sentence (the top bread/bun), supporting ideas (meat, cheese and/or vegetables in the sandwich), and a concluding sentence (the bottom bread/bun).

D. Next, you might like to have the learners help you write a model persuasive paragraph about your topic (See Strategy #48).

E. Then help students brainstorm topics for their own persuasive paragraphs. What is something that they'd like to try to get someone else to think or do?

**2.** Model the development of a persuasive argument.

**3.** Students outline their paragraphs with the sandwich organizer based on the reading selection.

**4.** Using their outlines, they draft and revise their paragraphs.

**5.** Finally, students share their finished paragraphs by reading them out loud to one another or the class.

**Example:** After reading and listening to the persuasive speech "Ain't I a Woman" by Sojourner Truth [https://youtu.be/XilHJc9IZvE;

http://en.wikipedia.org/wiki/Ain't_I_a_Woman%3F], learners analyze the speech and then use the Persuasive Essay Sandwich to outline their own persuasive essays.

# 37

# PROBLEM-SOLUTION CHART

| Problem-Solution Chart | |
|---|---|
| Text:<br>Author: | |
| **Problems** | **Solutions** |
| #1 | |
| #2 | |
| #3 | |
| #4 | |
| **Analysis:** The best option is _____ because: | |

This graphic organizer helps learners focus on the problems addressed and the solutions considered in a text. Then, students analyze the choices to find the best solution. This graphic organizer can also be used by learners to outline their own problem/solution writing, or when discussing an actual problem they face and coming up with solutions.

**Target Learning Strategies:** analyzing problems and solutions in a text

**Lesson Stages:** Into, Through, Beyond

**Language Levels:** All

**Procedure:**

1. Explain that learners can use this chart in describing problems and solutions in a text.
2. Discuss a problem in your life, for example, how to fit too many things into your schedule.
3. Have learners brainstorm possible solutions.
4. Analyze the solutions and conclude which is the best.

**Example:** In the example below, students outlined the problems described by Shawn Bradley in his essay "On Being Different" [http://usa.usembassy.de/etexts/soc/ijge0105.pdf pp. 14-15.] They then outlined the solutions offered and analyzed them to choose the best option.

## Problem-Solution Chart for "On Being Different," by Shawn Bradley

**Text:** On Being Different          **Author:** Shawn Bradley

**Main Problem:** Bradley has been extremely tall all his life.

| Problems | Solutions |
|---|---|
| #1 When he was small, he was not allowed on a carnival ride with his friends because he was too tall. | Bradley's mother realized the situation and explained it to the operator. |
| #2 When he was young, no one would believe his age. | Bradley carried his birth certificate everywhere. |
| #3 Other kids would challenge him to fight. | Bradley learned that he was important and loved, and this gave him strength to cope. |
| #4 Other teens would tease him, harass him, and laugh at him. | Bradley recognized that others were jealous and ignorant, and tried to understand them and not let what they did bother him. |

**Analysis:** The best option for Bradley was to use help from his family, his religion, and his friends to be strong and brave to not let what other people did hurt him.

# 38

# T-CHART/TABLE/MATRIX

**T-Chart**

A T-Chart, Table, or Matrix is a graphic organizer used for describing and/or comparing two or more things. For example, a T-Chart might be used to organize reasons for/against in an argument, or for outlining two different viewpoints on a topic. Examples include: pros and cons; facts and opinions; advantages and disadvantages; or strengths and weaknesses. A T-Chart can provide learners with alternate ways to show their understanding of what they have learned (Klingner, Hoover, & Baca, 2008).

**Target Learning Strategies:** reviewing key ideas and details; creating a drawing; elaboration

**Lesson Stage:** Beyond

**Language Levels:** All

**Procedure:**

1. Demonstrate making a T-Chart on the board.
2. Ask learners to draw a large "T" on their papers.
3. Guide them as they label the two columns, for example: advantages/disadvantages; pro/con; facts/opinions; strengths/weaknesses; or similarities/differences.
4. Model finding items to categorize under one of the two labels. Learners can complete the chart alone or in a small group after reading the selection.
5. Compare charts with others in the class.

**Example:** Students study the video *Energy and Matter*. http://studyjams.scholastic.com/studyjams/jams/science/matter/energy-and-matter.htm

| Energy: The ability to move or cause change in matter | |
|---|---|
| Potential | Kinetic |
| Possible or stored energy | Releases potential energy |
| Food can store chemicals as potential energy. | Thermal energy (heat) is an example. |
| When an electrical machine is waiting to be used | When an electrical machine is being used |
| An object on a shelf waiting to fall is potential energy. | Sound is kinetic energy. |

# 39

# TIMELINE: SHOWING CHRONOLOGY

| Timeline | |
|---|---|
| Dates, ages or other time divisions | Events |
| | |
| | |
| | |
| | |
| | |
| | |

A timeline helps learners organize events from a text into time order. It can be useful in summarizing a text or in discussing historical events.

**Target Learning Strategies**: reviewing key ideas and details; creating a drawing; elaboration

**Lesson Stage:** Beyond

**Language Levels:** All

**Procedure**

1. On the board, demonstrate creating timeline with your school schedule, or another familiar time sequence.
2. Help learners develop their own timeline of something recent, for example, events in the school year.
3. Explain that learners can use the timeline to outline events in the order they happened in a text.

**Example:** In the example, after studying dinosaurs using a variety of sources [e.g., http://dinosaurjungle.com/dinosaur_facts_timeline.php], each student chose a favorite dinosaur and placed it on the Dinosaur Time Line.

| Dinosaur Timeline | | |
|---|---|---|
| **Period** | **Leader** | **Events** |
| Triassic 250-200 million years ago | Coelophysis | 240-230 million years ago |
| Jurassic 200-150 million years ago | Stegosaurus Allosaurus Brachiosaurus | 160-150 million years ago 140-120 million years ago 70-60 million years ago |
| Cretaceous 150-50 million years ago | Ankylosaurus | 150-14 million years ago |

# PART V

## VOCABULARY EXPLORATION AND STUDY

Most learners of English are clear on one thing they need more of: words. Other aspects of the language (grammar, discourse, pronunciation, and social uses of language, to list a few) are crucial as well, but students perceive no other need as clearly as they do vocabulary. However, there are over a million words in the English language [http://languagemonitor.com]! Which words should we teach? And how?

Teachers have a central role in many aspects of vocabulary acquisition: motivating learners to want to learn new words; selecting highly useful academic words for direct teaching and practice; making learners aware of words and of aspects of words they encounter; developing learners' ability to use skills and strategies to analyze and learn about words on their own; and helping learners create and take advantage of opportunities inside and outside school to expand the depth and breadth of their vocabulary knowledge (Levine & McCloskey, 2013).

Three categories of words are particularly important and particularly difficult for English learners:

- academic words–words beyond the most frequently used 2000 found across academic texts in different areas;
- vocabulary specific to a content or discipline–"brick" words
- and what Dutro and Moran (2003) call "mortar" words–the general utility words and phrases required to construct academic texts, including connecting words, prepositions and prepositional phrases.

A useful tool for analyzing vocabulary of a text to select important terms to teach is the Vocabulary Profiler [http://lextutor.ca/vp/eng/]. If you insert a text into the engine, you can learn which words are most frequent, which are "academic words" (according to Coxhead's 2000 list), and which are "off list" words–often either technical terms or more rarely used ones.

Once you have determined what words are most important, this section offers strategies to introduce new words, explore meanings in depth, and provide practice for students to truly own the words.

**39. Conga Line/Inside-Outside Circles**: Learners practice terms with partners in lines or circles moving in opposite directions.

**40. Cooperative Sentences**: Learners work in a team to compose sentences in answer to questions–with each person contributing a word at a time.

**41. Direct Teaching of Vocabulary**: Teachers introduce important new terms in a series of steps intended to provide learners with deep interaction with the words.

**42. Drawing with Words**: Learners use words in drawings that show their meanings.

**43. I Have—Who Has?**: Learners practice terms, pronunciation, and meaning in a fast-paced game.

**44. Numbered Heads**: Learners answer questions in cooperative groups in which everyone is responsible and accountable.

**45. Personal Dictionaries/Glossaries**: Learners develop their personal lists of words and meanings to use and study.

**46. Think, Pair, Share and Variations**: Learners reinforce what they are learning by discussing it with partners.

**47. Word Solving**: Learners use a flow chart to deal with new words.

**48. Word Sort**: Learners explore relationships among words.

**49. Word Splash**: Learners make connections between words as they explore their meaning.

**50. Word Square**: Learners explore a variety of aspects and relationships among new words.

**51. Word Web**: Learners arrange words graphically to show relationships and meaning.

# 40

# CONGA LINE/INSIDE-OUTSIDE CIRCLES

Conga Line is a vocabulary game named after a popular Cuban line dance. The game provides a highly interactive way to study and review important terms. It helps learners develop vocabulary as they practice asking and answering questions.

Students form two lines (or two circles) facing each other and take turns asking and answering questions about vocabulary words or comprehension questions about readings.

**Target Learning Strategies**: practicing asking and answering questions; study strategies

**Lesson Stages**: Into, Beyond

**Language Levels:** All

**Procedure**:

1. Choose terms that have been recently taught, or review words.
2. A day ahead, each student prepares one or more cards, each with a term on the front and the definition, description, and example or picture) on the back.
3. Collect and check the cards, and then edit or ask for revisions to make sure that the information on each card is accurate.
4. Return the cards and have learners carefully study their cards to be prepared to teach their items to someone else.
5. Learners stand opposite partners in two parallel lines. Each learner has a different word card. At a signal, learners take turns teaching the partner opposite them the word on their card.
6. At the next signal, the two partners exchange cards. Then the last student in one line goes to the front of that line and everyone in that line moves back one.
7. At the next signal, the new partners teach one another

their new terms. This pattern continues until everyone
has partnered with everyone else.

8. Quiz learners on the words and set aside those that have
been mastered.

9. Play again (perhaps) another day with the words that still
need study or a different set of words.

10. *Optional*: Play conga music to signal time to change
partners.

**Variation: Asking and Answering Questions.** Use the
same procedure, but this time each student makes a card with a
comprehension question about a selection they have read. The
cards have the question on the front and the answer on the back.

**Example**: To practice for a test, assign each student a key term
from the topic. Students each write one question and answer
about the topic that includes or uses the meaning of the term.
Use these questions and answers for the conga line.

## 41

# COOPERATIVE SENTENCES

This cooperative learning strategy is an entertaining way for
learners to review information they have read while they learn to

construct sentences to ask and answer questions (Stack & McCloskey, 2008). Learners create a "sentence machine" to answer questions about a text in complete sentences—but each learner speaks only one word of the answer at a time. As a result, learners have to think "on their feet" about the answers, but also about many aspects of language—including grammar, collocation (what words "go together"), and word choice.

**Target Learning Strategies**: summarizing; synthesizing; reviewing; retelling; using physical action to remember language; word order and syntax

**Lesson Stage**: Beyond

**Language Levels**: Intermediate to Advanced

**Procedure**:

1. Ask students to work in groups of four. Have each group write three open-ended questions about the text they have read. Questions may be general or directed to a particular character in a story. (Note: some characters can be imaginary—even inanimate objects.)
2. Each group then sends one representative to stand in the front of the room.
3. Representatives stand in a line facing the class.
4. Have the line answer questions with sentences, each person speaking one word at a time (when an unfinished sentence gets to the end of a line, it "wraps" around back to the first). Use counting and general questions to help students get started. For example, ask, "What is your name?" Students answer the question in a complete sentence, one word at a time, for example, student #1 says "My", student #2 says "name", student #3 says "is", student #4 says "(her first name), student #5 says "(his last name)."

5. Invite a student from one of the groups to ask one of their questions. If the question is addressed to a character, remind the student to name the character.

6. Students in the front of the class answer the question in complete sentences, one word at a time. (Especially at first, the group will need considerable modeling and prompting from the teacher and other group members. Note issues of grammar, word choice, and word endings that will be valuable "mini-lessons" for the future.)

7. Continue until all questions are asked and answered.

8. **Variation:** For beginning and early intermediate learners, provide language frames for constructing both questions and answers: *Why did you _____ ? I _____ ed because _____.*

**Example:** After reading and studying any topic or selection, have students create questions about the main ideas and sequence of the story, then form a "sentence machine" to answer the questions in complete sentences by taking turns, each person adding one word.

# 42

# DIRECT TEACHING OF VOCABULARY

*Adapted from: Levine & McCloskey (2013)

**1. Present, pronounce, and define the word.** If the word can be illustrated, point to a picture that shows the meaning of the word. Write the word so students can see. Pronounce it and say, in simple terms that students can understand, what the word means. Whenever possible, present the word in a context that is meaningful and known to the learner.

*Our new term is* **geographical feature**. *Geographical features are the parts, or components, of the earth. Let's look at this globe/map. Mountains, oceans, rivers, deserts, and plains are all geographical features. Help me point to these geographical features. What kind of geographical features do we have where we live now? What kinds of geographical features did you have in places where you used to live?*

Use translations when available and helpful. Sometimes it is more efficient to help the learner grasp the meaning quickly by using his or her L1.

**2. Help the learners read and pronounce the word a**

**number of times.** Have learners count the syllables in the word and tap out the syllables on their desks. Include action games, call and response, and other techniques to make this activity lively and motivating.

*Ok, everyone, let's read this word:* **geographical feature**

*Say it in parts: geo—graph - ical - fea - ture*

*Say it backwards: ture - feature… ical - feature… graphical - feature… geographical feature*

*Say it quietly: geographical feature*

*Say it loudly:* **geographical feature**

*Say it slowly:* **g e o g r a p h i c a l f e a t u r e**

*See how you smile and hold your mouth open a little when you say that* **ee** *sound?*

*See how your lip touches your teeth when you say the* **ph** *sound?*

*Left side of the room, say the word:* **geographical feature.** *Now right side.*

*Whisper* **geographical feature** *to the person next to you: geographical feature*

## 3. Provide examples of the word used in several different contexts. Begin with familiar contexts and add newer and more sophisticated contexts as learners' knowledge of the word develops. Check comprehension with many questions.

*The most important* **geographical feature** *where I grew up was a* **lake.**

*The* **Grand Canyon** *is a beautiful* **geographical feature.**

*The **oceans** are the largest **geographical features** of the earth.*

*What do you think? Is a **dog** a **geographical feature?** A **peninsula?***

**4. Have learners create their own visual representations of the target word.** They may choose to use pictures, word squares, word circles, a semantic map, or other graphic organizers. Have them keep notes on important words in their personal dictionaries.

**5. Discuss features of the word**: other forms or parts of the word, and how the word is and is not used: *How many syllables are in this term? Did you notice that in this word, the f sound is spelled **ph**? Does anyone know a term like this in another language they speak?*

**6. Carry out many activities that help learners engage with the word.** Activities should progress from less demanding (such as signal responses) to more active participation with oral and written responses. Games and activities should provide a variety of encounters with the word that lead to rich, deep understanding. Help learners find ways to use the word appropriately in the classroom context, and celebrate when they do so. *Now I'm going to say some words. Put your thumbs up if the word is a geographical feature; thumbs down if it is not.*

**7. Have learners create their own visual representations of the target word.** They may choose to use pictures, word squares, word circles, a semantic map, or other graphic organizers. Have them keep their notes on important words in their personal dictionaries or on their personal word walls (see next page).

## 8. Discuss various aspects of the word:

a. Alternate forms of the word, for example, for the word hope:

| noun | hope, hopes |
|------|-------------|
| verb | hope, hopes, hoping |
| adjective | hopeful |
| adverb | hopefully |

b. Alternate parts of the word, for example, for the word *contradiction*:

*contra* (against) *dict* (speak) *tion* (noun ending)

c. How the word is and is not used:

We say: *make a mess*, not *do a mess*.

d. Other interesting features of the word, for example, that it has a homophone:

Site *is pronounced just like* sight. *Isn't that interesting? How are the meanings different? Can you think of a sentence that uses both words correctly? What is special about a website?*

# 43

# DRAWING WITH WORDS

Drawing with Words is a comprehension strategy that helps
learners to create mental images while a text is being processed

and to learn and study important words in the text. This strategy works especially well with texts include a lot of description and/or imagery. In this process, readers connect what they read with their own experience and create mental images that represent their understanding of the text. Unlike other activities where learners are encouraged to draw and describe images, here they share them by graphically presenting the text in a way that shows its meaning (Goldstein, 2008).

**Target Learning Strategies:** using imagery; using background knowledge; selecting and using key words

**Lesson Stages:** Through, Beyond

**Language Levels:** All

**Procedure:**

1. As learners read a text, ask them try to create mental images of the setting and events.
2. After they finish reading, ask them to draw the image, using whatever drawing materials you have (pencil, pen, markers, colored pencils...). Instead of line drawings, have learners use letters to create the shapes of their images. So, for example, the word *tree* would be repeated in the shape of a tree. Encourage learners to be as specific as possible when creating the word images. If learners work with computers, different fonts can be used to suggest aspects of objects.
3. Alternately, the drawing can be done as a whole class activity, with each student contributing a word or words to the class picture.
4. When the drawings are complete, have learners work in pairs to describe their images (or the class image) to one another. Then ask them to show how the images come

from the story, and to find similarities and differences among their images.

**Example**: Have learners create word pictures from a word or line in a poem, such as "The Road Not Taken," by Robert Frost [https://www.poetryfoundation.org/poems/44272/the-road-not-taken].

# 44

# "I HAVE – WHO HAS?"

The "I have–who has?" activity is a way to practice vocabulary, literature, or content concepts. This activity helps students reinforce a particular skill by matching a word with a definition or a question with an answer. It is a quick-paced activity that requires everyone in the class to participate in each round and leads to mastery of paired associations.

**Target Learning Strategies**: Vocabulary development; memorization; paced practice

**Lesson Stages**: Into, Beyond

**Language Levels**: All

**Procedure**:

1. After teaching new vocabulary or concepts, prepare a set of vocabulary cards by writing one of the new terms on each card with the statement "I have _____. On the bottom of the card, write the definition for one of the other vocabulary words with the stem "Who has…?"

(see samples below). The word and the definition on each card should not match. However, each word should have a definition on the next card in the set.

2. Make enough cards so that each student in the class has at least one card.

3. Pass out one or more cards to each student. You must use all the cards in the set when playing the game. If there are more cards than students, give some students two cards.

4. Give students a few minutes to look-up or check their notes for the definition for their "I have" word.

5. The first student says, "Who has…" and reads the definition on his/her card.

6. The student with the word that matches the definition says, "I have …" [the word].

7. This student now reads the definition on his/her card, "Who has …," and someone answers, "I have…"[word].

8. Play until all words have been defined.

9. Exchange cards and play the game again.

**Example:** Below are a few sample "I Have–Who Has?" cards to use with a science study of matter and energy. A template for creating cards can be found at: http://mlmcc.com/docs/I have Who has Template 24.docx

| I have the **first card**.<br><br>Who has *force*? | I have *a push or a pull*.<br><br>Who has **work**? | I have **when a force makes something move**.<br><br>Who has *friction*? |
|---|---|---|
| I have *a force that slows things down*. | I have *a force that pulls things toward the center of the earth*. | I have *the ability to do work*.<br><br>I have the **last card**. |

# 45

## NUMBERED HEADS

This powerful and engaging cooperative learning strategy (adapted from Kagan, 2004) can be used at many stages of a lesson: for brainstorming, problem solving, preview, or review. It effectively involves every learner and provides a structure for learners to support one another's achievement. In the example below, the questions are used in the "beyond" stage of the lesson to help learners intensively re-read a passage to find answers to questions.

**Target Learning Strategies:** summarizing; synthesizing; cooperating with classmates; inference

**Lesson Stages:** Into, Through, Beyond

**Language Levels:** All

**Procedure:**

1. Have students work in groups of about four.
2. Students in each group number off from 1 to 4. (If groups have 5, two students take turns as one number; if groups have 3, one student has two numbers.)
3. The teacher asks one question at a time about the text or topic and gives a time limit for the group to decide on an answer.
4. Group members "put their heads together" to find and agree on their answers. (This may include looking up page citations in a text, solving a problem, summarizing a passage, drawing a diagram, inventing a product...).
5. The teacher calls a number to designate which student will answer for the group.
6. Students with that number give their group's answers (orally, on paper, or on the board).
7. Give feedback as appropriate; teams might receive points for correct answers, creative answers, correct spelling, etc.

**Example:** Numbered Heads questions are used with a selection called "How a Bicycle Works," by Sharon Fabian [http://edhelper.com/ReadingComprehension_54_3283.html]. Students use both written text and illustration as sources for their answers.

- *What are the parts of a bicycle?*
- *How does a bicycle work? What makes it go?*
- *What are gears for?*
- *What did the first bicycles look like?*
- *Think of a question about the book for another group to answer.*

# 46

# PERSONAL DICTIONARIES / GLOSSARIES

Personal dictionaries empower learners by helping them choose target words and learn their meanings, uses, and/or spellings (Hart, 2009).

**Target Learning Strategies**: word analysis; vocabulary expansion; classifying vocabulary into meaningful groups; translation

**Lesson Stages**: Into, Beyond

**Language Levels**: All

**Procedure**:

1. Students can make their own personal dictionaries in a variety of ways:
2. They can use the last 26 pages in their journals, with a letter of the alphabet at the top of each page. They can use paper in their notebooks with initial letters, or index cards punched with holes to be put them in a binder. They can simply use a single ring to clip together pages or cards with a hole punched in them.
3. A Word Square can be used for each new word entry (see the "Word Squares" strategy).
4. Or, students can organize their words thematically (all the new words from something they read on one page, or words for a particular content area or topic in one section, or perhaps just words in the order they are added to the dictionary).
5. When students ask for the meaning or spelling of a word, or show they don't understand an important word, have them make an entry for that word in their personal dictionaries. Along with providing definitions and explanations, encourage them to use learner dictionaries, picture dictionaries, or other word sources to help them with the words.
6. Each entry should include information to help students

understand the words, i.e., the word, its pronunciation, its meaning in language the learner can understand, a translation, a sentence showing the meaning and use of the word, and/or an illustration.

7. Encourage students to work in pairs to practice and test one another on their words. If they forget how to spell a word, refer them back to their dictionaries. Periodically assess student understanding of their words, and have them check off words they've mastered and add new words they need to study.

**Example**: As they read about Ernest Shackleton and the Lost Antarctic Expedition, a nonfiction adventure story, from several sources [e.g., http://qa.timeforkids.com/node/136711/print], learners create entries for important words in their personal dictionaries using a table like the one below. (We've included a sample from the "C" page of a sample alphabetical dictionary.)

| Word | Definition/Translation | Sentence |
|------|------------------------|----------|
| chronological | In time order<br>*cronológico/a* | To make a timeline, I list events in chronological order. |
| covered | traveled, gone<br>*recorrida* | We walked for a week and only covered ten miles. |

# 47

# THINK, PAIR, SHARE AND VARIATIONS

Pair-Share structures offer learners the opportunity to think, listen, and respond to their peers. They gain a shared sense of meaning of the text (Snow, Burns, & Griffin, 1998), connect their own experience to new information, and gain from the experience of their peers as well, all as they negotiate meaning (Swain & Lapkin, 2000).

**Target Learning Strategies**: self-evaluation; practice and elaboration; writing a summary

**Lesson Stages**: Into, Beyond

**Language Levels**: All

**Procedure**:

**Into** the lesson: Ask pairs a previewing question to activate prior knowledge, for example, "What do you think will happen to the main character?" "What would happen if...?"

**Beyond** the lesson: Ask pairs a comprehension question or an opinion question, for example, "How would you summarize the story?" or present a problem to be solved.

**Procedure** for **Think, Pair, Share**

1. *Think*: Students think about the question and relate their own experience and ideas.
2. *Pair*: Partners take turns exchanging their ideas and listening carefully.
3. *Share*: Pairs share their answer with the whole class or with another pair of students. Each person shares his/her partner's ideas.

**Procedure *for Think, Quickwrite, Pair, Share***

1. After *Think*, add:
2. *Quickwrite*: Students write about their response for 5 minutes without stopping. Assure them that spelling and

grammar are not so important in this activity because this is a quickwrite. It's more important to get the idea down on paper than to have it be perfectly written.

3. *Pair*: Partners read what they wrote to their partners as partners listen; then discuss.

4. *Share*: Each pair joins another pair to form groups of four. Students take turns telling the group their partner's ideas. A few individuals then share their partner's ideas with the class.

**Example** of Think, Pair, Share: Students research the origin of their names on the Internet [http://behindthename.com] and/or by interviewing family members, and pair and share what they have learned to prepare to make a poster, a slide show, a prezi [https://prezi.com] or voki [http://voki.com] about their names.

# 48

# WORD SOLVING: NEW WORD DECISION-MAKING FLOW CHART

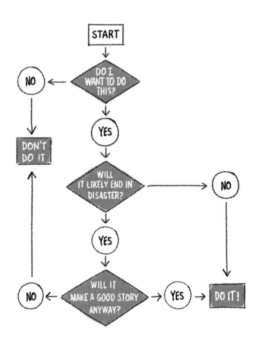

This graphic organizer (see next page) will help you introduce the many strategies available when a learner encounters an unfamiliar word.

**Target Learning Strategies:** solving unfamiliar words, word analysis, vocabulary expansion,

**Lesson Stages:** Into, Through, Beyond

**Language Levels:** Intermediate and Advanced

**Procedure:**

**1.** Introduce each element of the flow chart separately, over several days or weeks, including these strategies for word solving:

- Determining if a word is important for understanding.
- Finding a glossed term listed or explained on the page or at the end of the book.
- Using contextual information (surrounding text, visuals, etc.) to make a good guess at meaning.
- Using syntax to determine what part of speech the word is and get meaning from this.
- Recognize familiar word parts (prefixes, suffixes, root words) and use that to make a good guess at meaning.
- Looking for cognates, and seeing if that gives information for a good guess.
- Asking peers for help at appropriate times.
- Using a learner dictionary, picture dictionary, online dictionary, or translation dictionary to look up a word.
- Asking for help from the teacher.

**2.** Introduce the chart, explaining that the diamonds are decision points and the rectangles are procedures.

**3.** Choose sample words from a current reading and have

learners take a "finger walk" through the chart, stopping at each decision point and answering the question about the sample word, then proceeding as directed.

**4.** Encourage learners to consult the chart when they are stuck on a word to see if there is any strategy that will help.

**5.** Encourage learners to "internalize" the strategies and use them whenever they read.

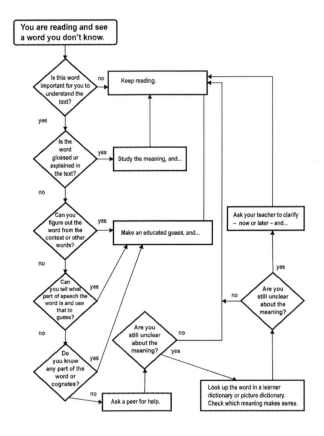

# 49

# WORD SORT

Word Sorts are instructional activities for studying words, word parts, and word relationships. These activities help learners both to look at words analytically and to develop an automatic reading routine (Tyner, 2004). Word Sorts guide students in the identification of common language patterns while engaging critical thinking skills. Two types of procedures and an unlimited variety of patterns in the English language create opportunities for many rich learning experiences.

**Target Learning Strategies:** selective attention; grouping; vocabulary study; classification

**Lesson Stages:** Into, Beyond

**Language Levels:** Beginning, Intermediate

**Procedure:**

There are two common procedures used for Word Sorts: closed sorts and open sorts. Each requires the application of different learning strategies by students.

## Closed Word Sort

1. Choose categories by which students will sort words from a reading selection—for example, by meaning, associations, vowel sound, initial sound, word family, final sound, prefix, suffix, root words, parts of speech, or initial letters in alphabetical order. Consider the level of the learners and important words in the selection.

2. Write the target words on cards or pieces of paper (or have students do this). On another color of paper, write the sort characteristics/categories that will be placed at the top of each column.

3. Have students place cards blank side up on the table. Then, working alone, in pairs, or in a small group, students select a card and place it under the appropriate sort category/characteristic.

### Example of Closed Word Sort

After reading "The Pasture," a short poem by Robert Frost, http://www.poetryfoundation.org/poems-and-poets/poems/detail/4427, learners study the new words in the story and then create a "word sort." Sample catagories:

| Nones | Adjectives | Verbs | Pronouns | Contractions |
|-------|-----------|-------|----------|--------------|
| pasture spring leaves water calf mother tongue | | | | sha'n't |

## Open Word Sort

In this activity, students determine for themselves how to categorize their words. Because an open word sort requires well-developed critical thinking skills, use this activity after students have had experience with a variety of ways to sort words.

Category suggestions for closed and open word sorts: sounds in words, prefixes, suffixes, and roots, parts of speech, meanings, word families, number of syllables, language roots, etc.

# 50

# WORD SQUARE

| WORD SQUARE | |
|---|---|
| **Word: Obstacle**<br><br>Translation: (Arabic)<br><br>عائق | **Symbol or Picture** |
| **My Meaning:** Something in the way.<br><br>**Dictionary meaning:**<br>Noun. Something that makes it difficult to achieve something (Longman Online Dictionary) | **My Sentence:**<br>The tree that fell across the road was an obstacle that cars couldn't pass.<br>Sentence from the selection:<br>"So I carry a (Rubik's) cube in my backpack as a reminder that I can attain my goals, no matter what obstacles I face." |

The Word Square graphic organizer (McCloskey & Stack, 2004) is a tool for multidimensional vocabulary development. Learners use a variety of ways to study a new term, including writing the word in English and their home language, writing a personal definition, writing a dictionary (or glossary) definition, using the word in an original sentence that shows its meaning, and drawing a picture of the word or action.

**Target Learning Strategies**: resourcing and transferring from L1 to L2, using inference; vocabulary study

**Lesson Stages**: Into, Beyond

**Language Levels**: Beginning, Intermediate

**Procedure**:

Draw a square on the board and divide it into four parts. Label each of the squares: *Word*, *Symbol or Picture*, *Meaning*, and *Sentence*. (Other possibilities: What the word does *not* mean, synonyms for the word).

Demonstrate by completing a Word Square with the whole class. Select a new word from a reading selection. Complete the square with the help of the class.

If using this graphic organizer during the **Into** part of the lesson, select important words for the reading and write them on the board. Students can work in groups or pairs on different assigned Word Squares, and then explain them to the class.

If you use this graphic organizer following the lesson, in the **Beyond** section, words can be self-selected or assigned and students can create their word squares independently or in pairs. Circulate the squares and let other class members offer feedback and suggestions.

Remind students that they can use this tool on their own with words that challenge them and that they can keep word squares in their Personal Dictionaries (Strategy #34.).

**Example:** Learners make Word Squares to study important words to prepare to read the essay "Accomplishing Big Things in

Small Pieces," by William Wissemann
[http://npr.org/templates/story/story.php?storyId=94566019].

# 51

# WORD WEB

Word Webs show relationships among words and can improve learners' understanding of both words and texts (Armbruster, Anderson, & Meyer, 1991). Word Webs are sometimes called semantic maps, brainstorming webs, or spider maps. They help learners make mental pictures of the relationships and connections among concepts and terms. The goals of this strategy are to expand and improve vocabulary used in speaking and writing and to increase comprehension in reading and listening through critical thinking about words and how they relate to one another.

**Target Learning Strategies**: word analysis; categorization; functional planning; grouping words

**Lesson Stages**: Into, Beyond

**Language Levels**: All

**Procedure**:

1. Select a main idea from the reading selection. Put that idea in a circle on the center of the board.

2. Ask students to give you words related to your main idea, and list the words on the side of the board. Students may need to consult a dictionary, a thesaurus, or an online tool like http://wordsift.com (this tool also provides images and examples to help learners understand new terms).

3. In the **Into** stage, you might accept any word related to the main idea. Offer your own input as well to expand vocabulary related to the chosen main idea.

4. In the **Beyond** stage, you might use word webs to check comprehension of the text and the vocabulary in the text by asking learners to give you only words and concepts from the selection.

5. Select sub-topics from your words.

6. Write these key words around your main idea, connecting them with lines. Now, add the words related to each key word around those key words and connect these words with lines.

7. As an extension, if appropriate to the topic, you can write short explanations showing the relationships on the connecting lines.

8. Encourage students to use the words in the Word Web to make statements about the relationships between the sub-topics and the main topic, for example, "Dillon is looking for a career. He wants to be a garbage collector or a fisherman."

9. When students understand the activity, they can work in small groups or as individuals to make their own word webs.

**Example:** Before reading the personal narrative "I am Kwakkoli," by Bisco Hill, from *Merlyn's Pen* [http://merlynspen.org/stuff/contentmgr/files/76a87ce759dcba

4c1268029797549efb/read/10.1.es.1.pdf], learners recall anything they know about a naming ceremony, and make predictions about what might be involved in such a ceremony. Then they work to fit words from the glossary on the Word Web.

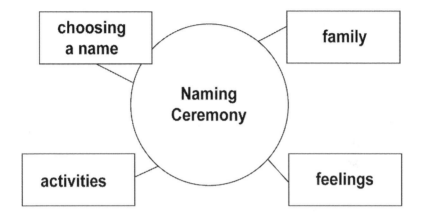

# REFERENCES

Aaronson, E. (n.d.) *The jigsaw classroom.* https://jigsaw.org/

Allen, J. (2002). *On the same page: Shared reading beyond the primary grades.* Portland, MD: Stenhouse.

Armbruster, B. B., Anderson, T. H., & Meyer J. L. (1991). Improving content-area reading using instructional graphics. *Reading Research Quarterly, 26* (4), 393-416.

Asher, J. (1966). the learning strategy of the total physical response: A Review. *The Modern Language Journal, 50*, 2: 79-84.

Bennett, E. (2004). *Connecting families to schools: Why parents and community engagement improves school and student performance.* New York: Fordham University, the National Center for Schools and Communities.

Brisk, M.E., & Harrington, M. M. (2007). *Literacy and bilingualism: A handbook for all teachers. Second Edition* Mahwah, N.J.: Lawrence Erlbaum Associates.

Buehl, D. (2008). *Classroom strategies for interactive learning (3rd ed.)*. Newark, DE: International Reading Association.

Bunch, G. C., et al. (2013). Realizing Opportunities for English learners in the common core english language arts and disciplinary literacy standards. (AERA Presentation).

Calderón, M. E. (2007). *Teaching reading to English language learners, Grades 6-12: A framework for improving achievement in the content areas.* Thousand Oaks, CA: Corwin Press.

Clay, M. M. (2001). *Change over time in children's literacy development.* Portsmouth, NH: Heinemann.

Cobb, T. (2015). The vocabulary profiler. (a tool for analyzing frequency and types of vocabulary in texts) http://lextutor.ca/vp/eng/

Cobb, T. (2015). Research base for the Compleat Lexical Tutor. http://lextutor.ca/research/

Coxhead, A. (2000). A new academic word list. *TESOL Quarterly, 34,* 213-238.

Coxhead, A. (2000). Academic Word List. http://www.victoria.ac.nz/lals/resources/academicwordlist/

Crystal, D. (1995). *The Cambridge encyclopedia of the English language.* Cambridge, U.K.: Cambridge University Press.

Dutro, S., & Kinsella, K. (2010). Language development: Issues and implementation at grades six through twelve. In *Improving California Department of Education: Education for English Learners: Research-Based Approaches.* New York, NY: Hippocrene Books.

Dutro, S., & Moran, C. (2003). Rethinking English language instruction: An architectural approach. In G. Garcia. (Ed.) *English learners: Reaching the highest level of English Literacy* (227-258). Newark, NJ: International Reading Association.

Fisher, D., & N. Frey. (2008). *Better learning through structured teaching: A Framework for the gradual release of responsibility*. Alexandria, VA: Association for Supervision and Curriculum Development.

Fountas, I. C., & Pinnell, G. S. (2016). *Guided reading. Second Edition: Responsive teaching across the grades*. Portsmouth, NH: Heinemann.

Freeman, D., Freeman, Y., Aurora Garcia, C. Gottlieb, M., McCloskey, M. L., Stack, L., & Silva, C. (2014). *On our way to English, 3rd Ed.* Austin, TX: HMH.

Gallagher, K. (2004). *Deeper reading: Comprehending challenging texts*. York, ME: Stenhouse.

Gambrell, L., Kapinus, B., & Wilson, R. (1987). Using mental imagery and summarization to achieve independence in comprehension. *Journal of Reading, 30,* 638–642.

Goldstein, B. (2008). Working with images. Cambridge, UK: Cambridge University Press.

Graham, Carolyn. (1993). *Grammarchants*. New York, NY: Oxford. Also available on Youtube: https://youtu.be/dT3kIBxmSBI.

Green, P, (Ed.). (1995). *Graphic organizer collection*. Palatine, IL: Novel Units.

Holdaway, D. (1979). *The foundations of literacy*. Sydney, Australia: Ashton Scholastic, distributed by Heinemann, Portsmouth, NH

Hyerle, D., & Hyerle, D. (2009). *Visual tools for transforming information into knowledge*. Thousand Oaks, CA: Corwin Press.

Jacobson, J., Johnson, K., & Lapp, D. (2011). *Effective instruction for English language learners: Supporting text-based comprehension & communication skills*. New York, NY: Guilford Press.

Kagan, S. (1994). *Cooperative learning*. Riverside, CA: Kagan.

Klingner, J.K., Hoover, J.J., & Baca, L.M. (Eds.).(2008). *Why do*

*English language learners struggle with reading?* Thousand Oaks, CA: Corwin Press.

Kress, J.E. (2008). *The ESL/ELL Teacher's book of Lists.* Jossey-Bass

Levine, L. N., & McCloskey, M. L., (2013). *Teaching English Language and content in mainstream classrooms.* New York, NY: Pearson.

McCloskey, M. L. (2017). Initial literacy development for learners of English. In J.I. Liontas (Ed.), *The TESOL Encyclopedia of English Language Teaching.* Hoboken, NJ: John Wiley & Sons, Inc.

McCloskey, M.L., Orr, J., Stack, L., & Kleckova, G. (2012). *American Themes: An anthology of young adult literature.* Washington, DC: Office of English Language Programs, Bureau Of Educational And Cultural Affairs, United States Department of State.

McCloskey, M. L., & Stack, L. (1996). *Voices in literature.* Boston: Heinle.

McCloskey, M. L., & Stack, L. (2004). *Visions: Language, literature, content—books A, B, & C.* Boston, MA: Heinle.

McKeown, M. G., Beck, I. L., & Worthy, M,J. (1993). Grappling with text ideas: Questioning the author. *The Reading Teacher 46,* 560–566.

Meyerson, M. J. & Kulesza (2010). The power of the language experience approach for struggling readers. In Meyerson, M. J. & Kulesza, D. L. (Eds.), *Strategies for struggling readers and writers.* New York: Pearson. Available: http://education.com/reference/article/language-experience-approach/

Nation, P., & Waring, R. (1997). Vocabulary size, text coverage, and word lists. In Schmitt, N., & McCarthy, M. (Eds.) *Vocabulary: Description, acquisition, pedagogy* (pp. 6-19). New York, NY:

Cambridge University Press. Available: http://lextutor.ca/research/nation_waring_97.html

Nieto, S., & Bode, P. (2012). *Affirming diversity: The Sociopolitical context of multicultural education* (6th ed.). New York: Pearson.

Oczkus, L. D. (2003). *Reciprocal teaching at work: Strategies for improving reading comprehension.* Newark, DE: International Reading Association.

Palenscar, A. S., & Brown, A. L. (1986). Interactive teaching to promote independent learning from text. *The Reading Teacher, 39*: 771-777.

Pearson, P. D., & M. C. Gallagher (1983). The instruction of reading comprehension. *Contemporary Educational Psychology, 8*: 317-344.

Raphael, V. (1986). Teaching question-answer relationships. *The Reading Teacher, 39*: 516-520

Rasinski, T. V. (2010). *The fluent reader: Oral & silent reading strategies for building fluency, word recognition & comprehension.* New York, NY: Scholastic.

Routman, R. (1994). *Invitations: Changing as teachers and learners K-12.* Portsmouth, NH: Heinemann.

Rutherford, B. (1998). *Instruction for all students.* Alexandria, VA: Just Ask Publications.

Sadler, C. P. (2001). *Comprehension strategies for middle grade learners.* Newark, DE: International Reading Association.

Samway, K. D., Whang, G., et al. (1995). *Buddy reading: Cross-age tutoring in a multicultural school.* Portsmouth, NH: Heinemann.

Saphier, J., Haley-Speca, M. A., & Gower, R. (2008). *The skillful teacher: Building your teaching skills, 6th Ed.* Acton, MA: Research For Better Teaching,

Snow, C.E., Burns, M.S., & Griffin, P. (Eds.). (1998) *Preventing reading difficulties in young Children.* Washington D.C.: National Academy Press

Soto, G. (2000). The marble champ. From *Baseball in April and Other Stories.* HMH for Young Readers.

Stack, L., & McCloskey, M.L. (2008). *Teaching tolerance through English.* Unpublished workshop handout. Bacau, Romania.

Strickland, D.S., Ganske, K., & Monroe, J. K. (2001). *Supporting struggling readers and writers.* Portland, ME: Stenhouse Publishers.

Swain, M. & Lapkin, S. (2000). Task-based second language learning: The uses of first language. *Language Teaching Research, 4*: 253-276.

Topping, K. J. (1995). *Paired reading, spelling, and writing: the handbook for teachers and parents.* New York, NY: Cassell.

Trelease, J. (2006). *The read-aloud handbook.* New York, NY: Penguin Books.

Tyner, B. (2004). *Small-group reading instruction: A differentiated teaching model for beginning and struggling readers.* Newark, DE: International Reading Association.

Van De Weghe, R. (2007.) Research matters: What kinds of classroom discussion promote reading comprehension? *English Journal, 96*(3), 86-91.

Venn, J. (1880). On the diagrammatic and mechanical representation of propositions and reasonings. *Philosophical Magazine Series 5.10 (59): 1–18.*

Wells, G. (1986). *The meaning makers: Children learning and using language to learn.* Portsmouth, NH: Heinemann.

Worthy, J., & Prater, K. (2002). The intermediate grades: 'I thought about It all night': Readers theatre for reading fluency and motivation. *The Reading Teacher, 3*: 294.

Wright, A. (1985). *1000 Pictures to copy for teachers.* Boston, MA: Addison-Wesley.

Zwier, J. (2004). *Developing academic thinking skills in Grades 6-12.* Menlo Park, CA: International Reading Association.

# ABOUT THE AUTHORS

**Mary Lou McCloskey**, who got her start as a teacher of school-age learners, works as Director of Teacher Education and Curriculum Development for Educo in Atlanta; as English for Speakers of Other Languages Specialist for the Global Village Project in Decatur; and teaches English language education at Agnes Scott College. She has written many series for English learners and professional books, chapters, and articles in the field and has worked with teachers, teacher educators, and departments and ministries of education on five continents – including long-term projects in Egypt and Central Europe – as well as 35 US states. She focuses on multiple aspects of education for school-age learners of English in diverse settings.

Amazon Author Page: https://www.amazon.com/Mary-Lou-McCloskey/e/B0034NFU6Y

**Publications:**

- *Teaching English Language and Content in Mainstream Classrooms*, Linda New Levine and Mary Lou McCloskey, Pearson Education, 2012.
- *Voices in Literature, Bronze, Silver, Gold*, Mary Lou McCloskey and Lydia Stack, Heinle & Heinle, 1996.
- *Leadership in English Language Teaching and Learning*, edited by Christine Coombe, Mary Lou McCloskey, Neil Anderson, and Lauren Stephenson, University of Michigan Press, 2008.
- *Visions A, B, C* and Ancillaries, Thomson Heinle, 2004. Sampler: http://ngl.cengage.com/milestonesvisionsfl/VisionsFLSamplerFtPlowres.pdf
- *On Our Way to English*, Donald Freeman, Yvonne Freeman, Aurora Colón-Garcia, Robert Marzano, Mary Lou McCloskey, Cecilia Silva, and Lydia Stack, Houghton Mifflin Harcourt, 2014.

‿

**Lydia Stack** is an internationally known teacher educator and author. She is currently involved in a Stanford University Initiative to support English Learners, *Understanding Language*. The goal of this project is to provide teachers with approaches to enrich academic content and language instruction for English Learners (ELs) in grades K-12. In addition, she presents workshops on peace, tolerance, and understanding to teachers in many countries around the world, most recently in Greece and Hungary.

Her teaching experience includes twenty-five years as an elementary and high school teacher of ELs in the San Francisco Unified School District and ten years as a district administrator. She is a past president of Teachers of English to Speakers of Other Languages (TESOL). Her awards include the TESOL James E. Alatis Award and the San Francisco STAR Teacher Award. Her publications include *Collections*, *On Our Way to English*, and *American Themes*, a literature anthology for high school students in the ACCESS program of the U.S. State Department's Office of English Language Programs.

**Gabriela Kleckova**, a language teacher, university lecturer, teacher trainer, researcher, consultant, and materials developer, is based in the English Department, College of Education, at the University of Western Bohemia in Plzen, the Czech Republic. In her 20 years in the profession, she has taught a wide range of general English courses as well as ESOL professional courses for pre-service and in-service teachers of various cultural and language backgrounds. Her main research interests include the effectiveness and utility of visual design of ELT materials. She is also interested in materials development, content and language integrated learning (CLIL), and teacher education.

**Janet Orr** is a highly experienced educator providing quality basic education program services for youth in both the United States and developing countries in Africa, the Middle East, and Asia. Janet brings a comprehensive knowledge of basic education programming especially in the areas of reading and English language learning. She has servèd in both US and overseas contexts as an administrator, curriculum developer, and teacher educator. Most recently, she is focused on consulting work to design effective instructional programs using research and data gained through program evaluation.